AWAKE AT WORK

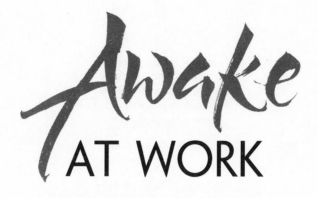

Awake
AT WORK

FACING THE
CHALLENGES OF
LIFE ON THE JOB

MICHAEL CARROLL

SHAMBHALA
Boston & London
2004

Shambhala Publications, Inc.
Horticultural Hall
300 Massachusetts Avenue
Boston, Massachusetts 02115
www.shambhala.com

9 8 7 6 5 4 3 2 1

First Edition
Printed in the United States of America

♾ This edition is printed on acid-free paper that meets the
American National Standards Institute Z39.48 Standard.
Distributed in the United States by Random House, Inc.,
and in Canada by Random House of Canada Ltd

Library of Congress Cataloging-in-Publication Data
Carroll, Michael, 1953 Nov. 7–
Awake at Work : 35 Practical Buddhist Principles for
Discovering Clarity and Balance in the Midst of Work's
Chaos—1st Shambhala ed.
p. cm.
ISBN 1-57062-983-8 (hardcover : alk. paper)
1. Job satisfaction. 2. Mind and body. 3. Centering
(Psychology) 4. Motivation (Psychology) 5. Self-care,
Health. 6. Job enrichment. 7. Awake at Work
(Organization) I. Title.
HF5549.5.J63C373 2004
650.1—dc22
2004003510

To my mother, Elaine, who first pointed the way

To my father, Thomas, who first taught me to do no harm

To my teacher, Chögyam Trungpa Rinpoche,
who introduced me to reality

CONTENTS

PART THREE
Working with Others

PART FOUR
Acting Precisely

APPENDIXES

ACKNOWLEDGMENTS

I AM DEEPLY GRATEFUL to my teacher Chögyam Trungpa Rinpoche for firmly and kindly presenting the Shambhala and Kagyu-Nyingma teachings so that someone like me could gain some understanding; to Dudjom Rinpoche and the Karmapa for inviting small children to play in their field; to Sakyong Mipham Rinpoche for encouraging all of us to step out; to Osel Tendzin, who told me the truth; to Khenpo Khatar Rinpoche for patiently instructing me in *lojong*; to David Nichtern, who ordered me to write this book; to Susan Piver-Browne for enjoying the adventure with such good heart; to Carol Williams for carefully helping me craft my views; to Peter Turner for having confidence beyond hesitation; to Eileen Cope for being clear and encouraging; to Josh Baran for helping others without expectation; to Eden Steinberg for being disciplined and patient; to Alan Schoonmaker for being a wise and delightful sage who can even make poker a path of insight; to Ben Roter, who taught me endless lessons throughout my business career; to Steve McCurry for showing me how to travel in Tibet; to Dr. Flavia Cymbalista for teaching me how to listen deeply to the wisdom of my body; to Jonathan McKeever, who never let the flag touch the ground; to Ellie Byrom-Haley, who brought elegance to the celebration; to Katherine Handin, whose courage and sharpness never waned;

ACKNOWLEDGMENTS

to Hayden Gesar Carroll, my son, for inspiring me and making me smile each morning. Finally, I will be forever indebted to my best friend, Susanna Lack, who is ever tender and powerful and never lets me off the hook.

AWAKE AT WORK

GETTING STARTED
Work's Invitation to
Wake Up

IN 1980, at the age of twenty-six, I set aside my worldly ambitions—and cashed in all my savings—to attend a Buddhist seminary in Alberta, Canada, led by the renowned Tibetan meditation master Chögyam Trungpa Rinpoche. In seminary we sat in meditation for seven to eight hours a day, studied Tibetan and Indian texts, and discussed timeless Buddhist teachings among ourselves and with Rinpoche. The training was rigorous and thorough, and the time spent in those long, regal stretches of the Canadian Rockies was delightful.

For me, a young, enthusiastic spiritual seeker, I felt that I had arrived at the inner sanctum. I was living the cloistered life, studying ancient teachings with a renowned master. Surely this was as momentous as life could get! I had left behind the world of materialism, and I was studying meditation techniques that would lead me to wisdom and bliss. However, despite my lofty ambitions, I was soon to discover that I was being trained for something much more practical and profound.

As the weeks passed I decided with firm conviction that I

wanted to devote myself to spiritual study and meditation for the rest of my life. I contemplated the details of such a venture. Where would I live? How would I pay the bills? What bills would I even have? Could I wander from place to place, or should I find a monastery to take me in? How would my girlfriend feel about my living the life of a monk? She'd probably be relieved, I thought. It was all very exciting. I was convinced I was making the right choice.

Toward the end of seminary, I requested a meeting with Rinpoche, and I planned to let him know my intentions. One could never be quite certain what he would say, but I was pretty sure that he would give me advice on how to proceed. Maybe he would suggest that I join a monastery or direct me to go on an extended meditation retreat. Maybe he would see my true potential and send me to Sikkim to study at the feet of the Karmapa, one of the most revered teachers of Tibetan Buddhism!

As seminary drew to a close, we all gathered for a graduation celebration. Rinpoche joined us for the festivities and took a seat at the far end of the large, spacious ballroom. That evening the sadness of the many farewells, the budding Canadian spring, and the graduation party were mingling into a perfect ending to a truly defining time in my life, when a young man said to me, "Rinpoche will see you now."

"Now," I thought. "In the middle of a party?" I finally had my chance to speak with him, but I didn't feel prepared.

I was escorted to Rinpoche and after the customary bow and then the typical silent, awkward moments, I began to explain my plans to become a full-time meditator. He patiently listened to my reasoning, smiling, nodding his head and studying my face. I explained to him that I had left my job, given up my home, and cashed in my savings to come to seminary.

I was devoted to getting to the heart of the teachings, committed to meditation, and prepared to spend the rest of my life focused exclusively on the Buddhist path. Now I just needed a little advice, a tip or two. So I asked: "How should I proceed?"

"Go home and get a job," he replied instantly. I stammered and tried to get my footing; my mind was racing. "Maybe he thinks I'm not good enough to be a monk. Or maybe he thinks I am someone else. That's not unusual; with so many students, he could make a mistake like that." I grabbed for a story line—any story line. I didn't expect him to tell me to get lost—to go get a job!

Then I thought, "Maybe I haven't been clear. Maybe he misunderstood me." I got control of myself and repeated my rationale once again. And again, Rinpoche patiently listened to my reasoning, sipping from his glass and sitting solidly in his chair. Finally he sat back and with a wide, mischievous grin said, "You can do it. Give it a try." The interview was over, and my monastic career was on the rocks. The tables had been turned, and I was, in many respects, out in the cold.

So it was with mixed feelings that I left Canada and returned to New York City. But my brief conversation with my teacher marked the beginning of a spiritual adventure more fulfilling than I could have imagined at the time. Instead of seeking out a monastic life, I was to live in New York and find my spiritual footing in the bowels of capitalism, on Wall Street. Here I would come to learn that what I thought was trivial, the so-called conventional world, was in fact sacred; and what I had considered profound, the "spiritual path," was simply my own naive fantasy. I was to learn my spiritual lessons at work, not in a monastery.

Throughout my twenty-two-year career on Wall Street and later in publishing, I gradually came to understand the wisdom of my teacher's instruction. The daily grind, the successes and failures, the hard work and stress, all gradually unfolded as a profound teaching. And central to that teaching was the realization that the spiritual path is nothing other than living our very life, fully and confidently, in the immediate moment—and that nothing can be excluded, especially not our jobs. Scrubbing a floor, writing an e-mail, leading a country, feeding a hungry child, are all noble steps we take on our path to becoming completely *who we are, where we are*. Work becomes our spiritual journey when our destination is no longer just becoming more successful or more wealthy or getting a paycheck, promotion, or job security, but when we also work to resolve a most fundamental question: Can we be at home in our lives—can we be open, honest, and at ease under all circumstances, moment by moment?

Being at ease with ourselves at work can be a challenge indeed, because, try as we might, we cannot control work. It is chaotic, fickle, and messy. We may have a passion for becoming a superb doctor or a dedicated teacher. Or we may work hard at being an effective lawyer or outstanding dancer. But somehow complications always seem to get in the way: malpractice insurance, rebellious students, tough bar exams, tired ligaments. Work is never quite what we expect, and being successful at our jobs is never as simple as we hope.

Work's untidy complications can be distressing, at times even alarming. Our work lives unfold amid countless uncertainties and upsets that leave many of us feeling disappointed, stressed out, and even under siege. Today's business culture would have us believe that such complications are mere roadblocks to achieving what *really* matters: a paycheck, promotion, profitability. Business requires, indeed, often fiercely demands, that the path to success be as smooth as possible.

But such is never the case. Success is often elusive and work *by its very nature* is unruly and at times unfair—and deep down we know it. We know that career troubles and conflicts are inevitable, that stubborn personalities and poor decisions are par for the course. Yet, oddly, we keep treating such difficulties as bothersome detours and unwelcome intrusions.

If we want work to be more than just an annoying imposition in our lives, if we are intrigued by the possibility of being both successful *and* spiritually engaged at work, we will need to pause and examine our basic attitude toward our jobs. Maybe we're missing something. Maybe problems arise at work not as interruptions or intrusions, but as invitations to gain real wisdom. Perhaps, in some sense, work's "complications" are exactly what we're looking for.

At first glance, such a suggestion may appear strange. Yet, if we examine work closely, we will notice that whatever gets messy with our jobs demands that we slow down and pay attention. The difficulties go to the front of the line, so to speak, and stare us straight in the face. But all too often, rather than responding with the resourceful attention that the situation requires, we dig in and resist.

Sometimes we resist in small ways. Maybe we avoid a difficult coworker or make a harsh remark under our breath: "Here comes that knucklehead Frank again." Sometimes our resistance becomes all-consuming: a lawsuit turns into a lifelong battle or an offhanded remark becomes an eternal grudge. By recoiling from any of work's problems, we inevitably find ourselves in hostile territory—often feeling lonely, imprisoned, confused, even at battle with our jobs, protecting ourselves from work rather than achieving its objectives.

The sober reality we face is this: resisting work's difficulties and hoping for smooth sailing is pointless. Work, indeed all of life, is often disappointing and uncertain, and it is futile to expect otherwise. Being hostile toward any of life's difficulties only amplifies our discomfort, and we end up at war with ourselves, arguing with our lives rather than living them.

I still work in the corporate world today, and I also teach Buddhist meditation and lead seminars on work as a spiritual practice. I often begin my seminars by asking participants to list three adjectives that best describe work for them. Inevitably, the responses are the same: "stressful," "discouraging," "difficult," "worrisome," "frustrating." Occasionally a few positive adjectives are thrown in such as "challenging," "stimulating," or "creative." But for the most part, work is experienced as a burden, a threat, an inconvenience—a place where we are held captive by life rather than free to enjoy it.

Fortunately, we can stop feeling imprisoned by work. We can stop hoping for smooth sailing, and we can stop experiencing work as hostile territory. We can, instead, discover a profound sense of freedom and fulfillment in our jobs. But in order to do such a thing we will need to make a simple and profound shift in how we engage work: *rather than resist, we will need to slow down and open up.*

Rather than rejecting work's difficulties as bothersome interruptions, we can instead acknowledge work, with all its complications, as an invitation to wake up and live our lives honestly and fully. From this point of view, the problems that arise in our jobs are not inconvenient speed bumps or demoralizing battles but valuable experiences worthy of our wise attention. We can learn to welcome whatever stares us in the face—whether disappointing, exhilarating, confusing, or routine—confidently and fully.

If we take a moment to slow down and open up to our work circumstances, we will discover that work is continually inviting us to help, not hide; to listen openly, not close up; to connect, not detach; to perfect our skillfulness, not put it in question. But in our impatience to succeed and become better, faster, and more profitable, we overlook the fact that work, with all its pressures and problems, is encouraging us to be engaged, resourceful, and alive—right here, right now. And, maybe that is what we've really wanted all along: to simply be *awake at work.*

Engaging our jobs intelligently and without resistance does not require that we redefine our entire approach to our livelihood. We can engage our jobs sanely and openly without giving up on success or disregarding our feelings or ambitions. What is required is surprisingly ordinary: simply to be *who we are where we are,* to subtly shift from *getting somewhere fast* to *being somewhere completely.* By taking such an approach, we discover not only a larger view of work but also a basic truth about being human: by genuinely being ourselves in the present moment, we naturally become alert, open, and unusually skillful.

When we are willing to shift from getting somewhere fast to being somewhere completely, we discover that we are not just making a living but we are living our lives on the job, right here, right now, in all the present moment's vivid and remarkable immediacy. When we are on the job completely, we do not forget to live our lives. Whatever comes along is not dismissed as an annoyance or an obstacle, or pursued as a comfort or relief, on our way to somewhere else. Whatever comes along *is our life,* and we actively appreciate it and respect it for being so.

To be awake at work is to acknowledge, maybe just briefly at first, that work only offers us the present moment, which is fleeting and fickle and constantly surprising. Work, with all its pressures and successes and confusion, unfolds on its terms not ours, and we can be awake as it unfolds or we can resist—a choice we can and will make moment by moment for the rest of our lives.

Whether we are rich or poor, Christian or Sufi, CEO or hairstylist, we can accept work's invitation to wake up. We can learn how to engage every aspect of our lives as a spiritual practice and in turn live life confidently without fear or anxiety. But in order for our lives and jobs to be just such a spiritual path, rather than a fortress or a prison or a vacation, we must be willing to set out deliberately on a journey. This book is an invitation to take such a journey. In many respects, these pages pass along my teacher's invitation to "get a job"—to gently lay down our resistance and explore who we are at work. We are invited to bring along any baggage we feel fond of: management techniques, religious preferences, career ambitions, credentials and qualifications. Some of us may travel light, others may bring along a caravan. Along the way, we may discard some of these items, or we may discover some of them to be more useful than we had ever imagined. We will learn such lessons as we go.

Besides being an invitation, this book will also serve as a guidebook. Many others have made this journey before and learned the terrain; their wisdom is available and useful. So this book passes along a few hints and suggestions. As in any guidebook, there are warnings of dangers on the road, suggestions on where and how to refresh ourselves, pointers on how to work with surprises, and an occasional reminder on where to find the most scenic views. But most important, this book instructs us in the disciplines of traveling the path.

In order for us to journey with inspiration and delight, we will need to work with our minds. By this I mean making a gentle, firm, and utterly powerful gesture toward ourselves, not just once but throughout the entire journey, a gesture that cultivates sanity and well-being each step of the way. This gesture is *mindfulness*, and it is central to our ability to be awake at work. Mindfulness, in Buddhism and many other spiritual traditions, is essentially learning to be fully alert and available in the present moment. Whether we are pouring a cup of tea, changing a lightbulb or a diaper, or holding the hand of a dying friend, we glimpse through our mindfulness that our life is happening *now* and cannot be taken for granted. By being mindful, we face the ordinary, fresh immediacy of our experience and discover that simply being human is profound beyond our hopes and fears and preconceptions. Such mindfulness will be our vehicle for traveling the path; it will show us how to move forward and to trust ourselves step-by-step, moment by moment.

So, we embark on our journey. Our work now becomes our frontier, and we become pioneers of the unfamiliar. Gradually, we can stop struggling with our jobs and begin exploring them as uncharted territory. We can learn to acknowledge that anything can and does happen at work—which can be both shocking and delightful. When the phone rings, we may notice the fresh mind that we bring to such a simple and immediate invitation. When our boss is upset and overbearing, life will be uncomfortable. But we may also notice that we are sharply alert and intelligent at such moments—if we are *mindful*. And, by just showing up at work, we may also notice that we have already begun our spiritual journey and work's invitation to wake up is staring us right in the face.

Cultivating Mindfulness at Work

Learning to be awake at work is straightforward and very practical. It is not wishful thinking; we can't just hope ourselves awake and leave the rest to chance, with the vague idea of attaining a state of bliss on the job. Nor is it some new "technology of the mind" that we enthusiastically inflict on ourselves and our colleagues. Awakening on the job is learning to drop our resistance and be intelligently and energetically alert to our lives at work. This process is very personal and demanding. It means learning to live our lives nobly and without fear, coming down to earth and into direct contact with our experience. This takes effort and discipline.

You may think of discipline as a boot-camp mentality or as a kind of punishment. Maybe discipline brings to mind images of denying yourself your favorite foods, running long distances, or saluting your superiors and performing your duty. However, in this case discipline is not punishment or denial or obligation. Rather, the discipline required to be awake at work is learning to be completely honest with ourselves and overcoming any pretense or deception about our work circumstances.

Such honesty requires that we approach our jobs with a sharp and clear-minded intelligence that is neither gullible nor hardheaded. Being disciplined at work requires that we stop kidding ourselves—stop trying to defend our jobs, our prestige, our smooth path to success—and commit to being attentive to and honest about our actual experience. This willingness sets the stage for engaging work skillfully as it unfolds, without trying to secure our well-being or gather false guarantees. Such honest discipline is the essence of mindfulness, and it does not simply appear but must be cultivated over time.

Buddhism has a rich tradition of mindfulness practices that have been developed and handed down from teacher to student for centuries. The most common practice taught in most schools of Buddhism and some non-Buddhist traditions is called *mindfulness-awareness* meditation, or sitting meditation. In sitting meditation we learn to be still, directly experiencing our minds and hearts and the present moment. We explore very precisely and gently who and what we are, gradually seeing through our self-deceptions, becoming aware of our experience, and glimpsing a fundamental wakefulness that is in fact always available. With sitting meditation we begin to relate directly with the simple power and flexibility of being ourselves right here, right now.

Sitting is deceptively simple: We sit up straight, either in a chair or on a cushion on the floor, and remain attentive in the present moment. Our eyes are open, our hands are placed gently on our thighs or in our lap, and our gaze is soft and slightly downward. We breathe normally and sit still. Essentially, this is all we do. Just sit. It seems very simple, but a lot goes on.

When we sit still, we will inevitably notice the vividness of the moment, even if for just a brief second. Perhaps we may notice the sound of a fan or the wood grains of the floor. Maybe we detect the faint echo of traffic off in the distance or sense the cool humidity of the rain gently falling on the roof. When we sit, we glimpse the simple, clear *nowness* of sights, sounds, and physical sensations.

We may also notice that we are thinking. We may be recalling a TV show that we found memorable or rehearsing a difficult conversation we are expecting to have with a loved one. Our thoughts may be restless and cranky, meandering and dull, or colorful and engrossing. This bright and shifting quality of the mind is not a problem; it is what we work with.

In sitting we attend to our thoughts and our sensations by cultivating a precise yet gentle awareness of the breath. When we notice we are thinking, we make a slight shift. We deliberately note our thinking and gently bring our attention back to our breath. In sitting meditation, we learn to lightly "ride" the breath in this way to stabilize our attention in the present moment. By sitting in such a way, we feel the rhythm of our minds and engage emotions and thoughts of all kinds. Rather than getting lost in our thoughts and emotions, however, we learn to touch our feelings and *let go*, bringing our attention back to our lives in the immediate moment, right here, right now.

Maybe you already have a mindfulness practice of some sort. If it is sitting meditation, you will probably be at home with many of the themes discussed in this book. If you are unfamiliar with mindfulness and meditation, that's fine, too, because now you'll have a chance to consider cultivating mindfulness in your life and especially on the job.

If you aspire to relate to work in a more open, wise, and enlivened way, I believe you will be greatly helped by taking up a regular sitting meditation practice. Many people before us have practiced sitting meditation and discovered a natural wisdom that transformed their lives, and such possibilities are open to us as well. For those who feel inspired to begin meditating, more extended instructions for getting started are offered in the appendix "Instructions for Mindfulness-Awareness Meditation." But whether you practice sitting meditation or not, the material offered in this book will help you engage your job with courage and candor. Being mindful in our jobs will teach us to trust our natural talents and rediscover a sense of well-being at work.

Of course, being mindful won't make our jobs any less messy. Cranky customers, computer viruses, and overly competitive colleagues don't suddenly disappear because we are mindful and alert to the immediate moment. And neither does our resistance to work's difficulties. We might still feel annoyed by "knucklehead Frank," who criticized our sales presentation, or uneasy at the prospect of losing our job or resentful toward our employer. Being mindful in the immediate moment will never eliminate work's real and never-ending problems or all our resistance to them.

But mindfulness does make us increasingly curious about our predicament. The more we attend to work in the immediate moment, the more our mindfulness begins to develop a keen edge of curiosity. We go about our jobs, but now we are more attentive to how work gets messy and how we resist. Our annoyance with our client or hesitations to be candid with our boss are no longer an irritating undertone but become sharply apparent and interesting to us. It's as if we're haunted by our heightened mindfulness. We are continually noticing more, pausing in the midst of the hectic pace, opening to the rawness of our daily work experiences, and becoming more and more candid with ourselves.

Developing mindfulness, then, is really our central task at work. But not because we prefer to develop ourselves spiritually rather than get the job done. Being mindful at work doesn't turn our jobs into a Himalayan retreat or a meditation cushion. In fact, mindfulness becomes central because we finally want to do our jobs properly rather than protect ourselves from work's unpleasantness. We are mindful at

rk—indeed, in our entire lives—because once and for all
∗ want to live life well, without anxiety and resentment.

In this book we will cultivate mindfulness on the job by
working with a set of thirty-five principles or slogans designed
to help us rediscover our natural wisdom, openness, and poise
as we engage work's daily demands. The slogans I offer are
inspired by a classical Tibetan Buddhist text called *The Root
Text of the Seven Points of Training the Mind* and its transforma-
tive spiritual practice called *lojong*. This text comes from the
eleventh-century Buddhist master Atisha Dimpamkara Shri-
jnana and at its essence it seeks to loosen our resistance to
life, ease our self-deception, and reveal the awakened state as
ordinary experience. Atisha's oral teachings were organized
into fifty-nine pithy slogans, shorthand instructions for cultivating compassion and wakefulness under any circumstances.
For more than a thousand years Tibetan Buddhists have
worked with these slogans as a daily spiritual practice, and
many of the great Tibetan spiritual teachers have commented
on the text, expanding and refining the practice.

The *lojong* slogans offer instruction that is extremely practical and to the point. They include "Be grateful to everyone,"
a reminder that those we meet in our lives are a great gift,
not a pincushion for our resentment or arrogance. Two other
penetrating slogans are "Don't wait in ambush" and "Don't
act with a twist." These counsel us to be alert to our own
hypocrisy and to be straightforward and decent in our dealings
with others. And one of my favorites is "Always meditate on
what provokes resentment," which reminds us to be particularly attentive to what upsets us and to explore carefully what
makes us feel threatened or disoriented.

Lojong practitioners commonly memorize all fifty-nine slogans or copy them onto wood, paper, or stone, placing them

in various locations where they can catch the eye. In this way the slogans are naturally recalled throughout the day, providing guidance. By keeping alert to the slogans, *lojong* practitioners permit daily events to evoke the slogans' natural wisdom, revealing ordinary experiences as extraordinary opportunities to wake up.

Having applied these traditional Tibetan Buddhist teachings on the job throughout my twenty-two-year corporate career, I became inspired to develop a set of slogans uniquely adapted for the modern workplace. As with the original *lojong*, the slogan practice I offer in this book provides a way to engage our work honestly and sanely, gradually learning to trust our innate wisdom and well-being as we perform our jobs.

The thirty-five slogans I present and discuss are concise and sometimes provocative reminders designed to help us to wake up on the job. I encourage you to work with these slogans as a contemplative exercise. Read and reflect on them at your own pace. Engage the themes and ideas they present, testing them against your own experience. While on the job, you may soon find yourself spontaneously recalling a slogan that offers insight into your immediate situation.

Let's take an example. We might look at the slogan "Welcome the tyrant." Essentially this slogan points out that colleagues at work can at times be irritating or threatening— even insulting. Normally, in such circumstances, we can find ourselves stewing with our resentments, pondering the insults and pressures. The slogan points out that by brooding in such a way, we actually create our tyrant; we author our own predicament. The slogan suggests that instead of fighting our tyrants, we might welcome them and, in so doing, learn vital lessons about ourselves and doing our jobs properly.

Now, let's say we read this slogan, maybe at home or on our

commute to work. We reflect on the slogan's meaning to see how our experience matches up. Maybe we recall a bitter conflict we're having with a colleague or remember how we fumed over some injustice at work. Maybe we think that the slogan is somewhat true but not really that relevant. Or maybe we say to ourselves, "That's exactly how it is for me at work! I'm creating my own tyrants." We reflect on our work lives, think about the slogan "Welcome the tyrant," consider our experience, then move on, maybe reading the newspaper or having a cup of tea.

At some point, however, we will find ourselves at work once again facing some mess, maybe an irate client, and we recall "Welcome the tyrant." The phrase may come unexpectedly to mind, or a physical feeling might remind us; in either case, the slogan mixes with our experience. It informs and sharpens our curiosity, and we begin to experiment, though maybe only briefly at first. Maybe instead of biting our tongue and quietly raging as our client complains, we will find ourselves a bit curious, thinking, "Hey, this guy is really upset. I wonder why? Maybe this is about more than our check being seven days late." Or maybe, as we notice that we are stewing, we recall "Welcome the tyrant," and suddenly the entire drama loses its edge, freeing us from the trap for just a moment. In this way our slogan practice becomes contemplation-in-action, and our work actually becomes our spiritual path.

It should be clear by now that the slogans aren't meant to be read as simple instructions or how-to advice. Instead, they come alive in our daily experience, becoming part of the atmosphere rather than a manual in our desk drawer. The slogans are meant to instigate change, strengthen our mindfulness, and encourage us to question the common assumptions that make us resist work and lose our natural sense of composure and well-being. Consequently we may sometimes find them repetitive, taking different yet valuable angles on the same issue. At times they may feel provocative or especially penetrating. The slogans are not a rule book or manual on what "good" awake-at-work behavior is—this is not an exercise in morality. Rather, the slogans are very practical. They are to be used like smelling salts that we apply in order to actually wake up at work.

Contemplating the Awake at Work Slogans

The Awake at Work slogan practice is not a one-shot deal, something we do once and then consider ourselves finished. Rather, it is a gradual path, a continuing process of learning how to engage work skillfully in the moment. The slogan practice is organized into four sections: "The Four Primary Slogans," "Developing a Composed Attitude," "Working with Others," and "Acting Precisely." I recommend approaching the book and the slogan practice as follows:

1. Study the four primary slogans first. Four fundamental reminders form the basis for the slogan practice. These are "Balance the two efforts," "Be authentic," "Cultivate *li*," and "Work is a mess." I highly recommend that you read and reflect on these four slogans before considering the other thirty-one.

2. Randomly select slogans. Once you have familiarized yourself with the four primary slogans, I suggest you randomly select other slogans to study. You do not have to read all the slogans in order, one after another. Glance over the table of contents and select a slogan that seems to be speaking to you,

or simply open the book randomly and begin reading the slogan that you find there. After finishing a slogan, take a brief moment to set the book aside and consider what you've read.

3. Watch how the slogans spontaneously arise at work. In the course of your job, events will most likely remind you of a slogan. When that occurs, be attentive; permit your natural curiosity to engage the situation as it unfolds. Pay attention to any physical feelings, letting them guide your thinking; observe how emotions and thoughts arise and dissipate; be mindful of how you and your colleagues are behaving. Experiment with the new perspective the slogan provokes. Has it created a shift in attitude? How does it feel to view work from a new angle? Have you behaved differently because of the slogan? How and what was the outcome? Permitting the slogans to mix in this way with your work *as* you work is highly encouraged.

4. Deliberately contemplate the slogans. You can also try studying the slogans more deliberately and systematically:

- Each morning, select a slogan for the day. Read it before beginning work, then look for ways to apply that slogan on the job.
- Keep a journal of your experiences and reflections about the slogans.
- Write a slogan onto your daily calendar where it will catch your eye throughout the day.
- Work with the slogans as a structured spiritual practice using the instructions offered in the appendix "Instructions for Contemplating the Slogans."
- Conclude sitting meditation sessions by reading and contemplating a selected slogan.
- Copy the slogans onto index cards and place a

selected slogan discreetly on your desk, by your computer, or near the phone as a way to have ongoing access to the slogan's guidance.

• Memorize all thirty-five so that you can more easily recall them at will.

Finally, it is important to remember that this slogan practice is simply provoking our natural intelligence. It is not proposing a new management technique or imposing a how-to or announcing an "eight-step method." It is tickling us, inviting us, challenging us to welcome and respect our jobs fully and thoroughly—to be *who we are, where we are* on the spot.

PART ONE

THE FOUR PRIMARY SLOGANS

The slogans in this section form the basis for the entire practice. In many respects the awake-at-work path can be summed up in these four slogans alone:

- Balance the two efforts
- Be authentic
- Cultivate *li*
- Work is a mess

When we mix these slogans with our daily work, we awaken our natural courage to engage our jobs in the present moment without fear or arrogance. We learn to trust our instincts to be kind and fair, and we recognize that our desire to succeed at work can be fulfilled only if we are willing, first, to be some-where completely. The four primary slogans point to the reality that *who we are, where we are right now* is unspeakably profound and noble. This truth is woven throughout the entire slogan practice.

1

Balance the two efforts

MANY OF US MAY remember the first time we rode a bicycle. I was around four years old, and my dad would take me out in the alley behind our home and show me how to peddle, steer, and apply the brakes. Since I had training wheels, I could feel a kind of confidence in my efforts, pretending to have balance and feeling my way. Eventually my dad removed the training wheels. He would run behind me holding the seat, keeping me steady and urging me on—slightly letting go, only to grab hold once again as I tilted to the right or left.

One morning after breakfast we went out to practice riding once again. We started at the end of the alley. My dad held on to the seat and guided me as we picked up speed. I'll never forget saying to him, "Boy, we're really going fast this time!" Not hearing a response, I turned toward him. There he was, way back at the other end of the alley, watching me triumphantly. I realize today that it wasn't really my dad who had let go on that morning. I had.

I had let go for the very first time. Let go of my fear of falling, my need for training wheels, even my desire to ride a bike. I had let go of my hesitations and trusted myself to be fully with the moment. For the first time in my life I had totally relied on myself—my natural sense of flexibility, alertness, and grace. I had learned balance.

This simple act of riding a bike for the first time has remained fresh in my mind through the years, for it perfectly illustrates how we can learn balance at work—or indeed in our lives. Our effort to get somewhere, whether in our career, in our life, or in simply riding a bike, depends on first *being somewhere*, letting go of our fears, desires, habits, and routines and trusting ourselves fully in the present moment. Trust that we can ride a bike without training wheels, trust that we can build a career without hope and fear, trust that we can live a life without resentment and complaint. In turn, we discover balance in simply being present and an alertness that is resourceful, flexible, and relaxed. By letting go of our hesitations and discovering balance, we learn one of life's great lessons: in order for us to *get* somewhere, we have to *be* somewhere first.

Work has a peculiar way of keeping us off balance, focusing us on the future, worrying about where we are going, concerned about whether we will arrive at our destination with our career and paycheck intact. Being out of balance in such a way—focusing mainly on getting somewhere—can make us feel hesitant, worried, and restless. We may feel alert at work but not as free and open as we sense we could be. We may be enthused by the challenge, yet we are cautious and uneasy. The old question "What keeps you up at night?" is quite literal in business. Will the new accounting system launch smoothly this weekend? Will the presentation to the division president go well tomorrow? Will I get the promotion or will I be passed over again? The *hecticness* of succeeding, measuring up, responding to emergencies, getting somewhere fast, can keep us living in constant anticipation, robbing us of any sense of well-being and enthusiasm, making work a burden and distracting us from our lives.

Ironically, focusing too much on the future may not help us achieve our goals as much as we think. When our efforts become singularly focused on getting somewhere, we become like athletes who exert enormous effort to achieve narrow results. If we lift weights and do push-ups to develop our upper-body strength, we might become expert in weightlifting; we might gain the ability to lift refrigerators and maybe pull trucks but not to deal with broader challenges. If we were asked to play a round of tennis or shoot an arrow accurately or perform a grand jeté in a ballet, we would be woefully ill equipped. The essential grace and flexibility would be missing.

In the same way, work presents us with challenges that demand different capacities than the tireless focus on getting somewhere fast. We cannot rely solely on muscle and will when facing work's challenges. Work often requires finesse and timing to see beneath the surface of a situation, apply creative imagination to an impasse, or build a bridge between colleagues. We don't access these abilities by speeding forward. We develop such abilities by learning to let go and be where we are completely.

Such "letting go" does not seek to measure up to an expectation or external standard. Letting go is not particularly strenuous, like lifting weights or painstakingly reviewing a complex balance sheet. Rather, it requires us to relax and open into the present situation, whatever it is, with no fixed idea or bias. It asks that we trust ourselves enough to loosen our hold on whatever is familiar and comfortable and leap into our natural sense of balance. By letting go we postpone the story lines and mental habits that we typically bring to our work and simply become available to our circumstances at that very moment—no matter how pleasurable or difficult they may be. We bring our naked curiosity to our work and permit the situation to unfold at its own pace and on its own terms. Letting go has no agenda other than to be thoroughly and intelligently available to our immediate circumstances, a gesture that demands flexibility, alertness, and grace.

"Letting go" might sound like some kind of glorified spacing out. We are very busy people. We have long "to do" lists, and letting go doesn't appear on them. We can let go in our spare time or on the weekend. We can ride a bike or "stop and smell the roses" on vacation. Surprisingly, letting go at work is much more than just taking time out to smell life's roses. In some cases it can be a matter of life and death.

A doctor's ability to be fully alert when diagnosing a health problem often spells the difference between vitality and disaster. Noticing a seemingly minor scratch or unusual prescription dosage can pique a physician's interest to look a bit closer and discover an impending health crisis. Physicians are trained to let go of their training as much as rely on it; being available to the circumstances as they unfold is very much the physician's territory. There are other professions where letting go of preconceptions and being fully present to circumstances as they unfold is absolutely vital: air traffic controller, fire fighter, emergency medical responder, teacher.

Actually, cultivating our ability to let go is essential to whatever kind of work we do, if we are to work to our full capacity. All of us have the ability, for example, to say or do just the right thing in the moment or produce useful ideas out of what seems to be thin air. While this ability comes naturally, it must also be cultivated. Like most elegant and powerful things, our ability to let go and *be* has its own inherent strength, but it also requires respect and care and nourishment.

In Buddhism we cultivate this natural ability to "let go" in mindfulness-awareness, or sitting, meditation. Sitting is traditionally considered a singular moment where we discover the balance between getting somewhere and being somewhere at the same time, like riding a bike. In sitting meditation we attempt to get somewhere—to develop calm minds and open hearts—by letting go of our constant verbal rehearsals and being fully with our situation as it unfolds. We learn that we can ride the present moment without the training wheels of story lines and preconceptions. In meditation we let go of our internal chatter hundreds of times—over and over and over again. Over time we discover a balance to our effort that is lively yet effortless; simple yet demanding. Just as an athlete's daily workout is central to performing on the court or field, regular meditation is the foundation for balancing effort and extending it to the job.

As we begin to practice regularly, we see that letting go happens quite simply in our lives. All we have to do is notice. We may be hurrying to our jobs in the morning, maybe on a crowded subway or through traffic. Ordinarily we would be preoccupied with thinking about our day ahead, perhaps a staff meeting, completing a report, or meeting with our manager. And then, suddenly, for no particular reason at all, we notice the person sitting across from us on the train. Just for a moment we linger and notice our neighbor's necktie and the care he has taken in having his shirt starched. We notice the pace of those around us—some glancing at their watches, others reading the paper, others rushing to get on and off at the station. We let go of our internal dialogue and find ourselves drinking in the entire moment fully and thoroughly, acknowledging, for a brief refreshing moment, that our world is tremendously open beyond our preoccupations.

Over time we begin to make friends with this simple ability to let go and be somewhere completely. We discover that if we try too hard to let go, we become distracted by our effort, peddling too fast, trying too hard. Or we may find that when we forget to let go, maybe for days on end, we end up relying too much on emotional training wheels, feeling anxious or stressed out. Gradually, through sitting, we find by being somewhere completely that we are inviting our world into our lives, which is a basically sane and respectful gesture. As with all invitations, we cannot force guests to arrive; we are just opening our lives, being available to whatever turns up in the present moment.

When we let go and become available to our work, we may notice, even just for a moment, that we are inviting a much wider and wiser perspective. Irritations that we may easily dismiss—the predictably late report, the sullen receptionist, the unresponsive customer—become reminders to pay attention. Routine moments like signing expense reports invite a renewed attention to detail. Because we are available, our work world becomes like our patient, where we are attentive and alert to signs of health and distress.

In letting go we are not adding anything to our "to do" lists. We are simply balancing the effort to get somewhere with that of being where we are completely, opening ourselves up to a much larger work perspective. Eventually this shift becomes quite routine, allowing us to reconnect with our natural intelligence—an immediate and extraordinary spontaneity and confidence—at will. By letting go over and over again, we reenliven our sense of well-being and become aware of an openness at work that does not need to be managed or arranged.

We gradually discover a composure that has been with us our whole lives but has somehow gone unnoticed.

"Balance the two efforts" reminds us that we can afford to drop our point of view for just a moment and listen to our world, no matter how tedious or threatening such a prospect may seem. Our ambition to succeed, our tight timetables, our authority, our "correctness"—all of it can, for a brief moment, simply be put on hold. We can then bring our uncluttered attention to our work's circumstances, inviting our world in and acknowledging the vastness and liveliness around us. By making such a gesture we learn balance—that we can actually get somewhere and be somewhere at the same time. Such balance is the height of gracefulness and authenticity. It is the core competency of being awake at work.

2

Be authentic

AS THE NOBLE twenty-five-hundred-year-old legend goes, the young and troubled Indian prince Siddhartha renounced his royal powers and worldly pleasures and left home. He cut his hair, donned mendicant's robes, and sought to liberate himself from life's suffering and to attain "enlightenment." Over the years, he practiced many yogic disciplines and meditations. He fasted to the extreme—almost to death—eating one hemp seed a day. He endured enormous loneliness and conquered enticements of all kinds in his attempts to unravel humanity's suffering. Yet despite his devotion and all his tireless efforts, he was left unfulfilled and restless.

And so, after eight years of discipline and hard work, Siddhartha decided to give up. He was not defeated, however; rather, he had decided to finally surrender everything, including his desire to escape suffering and attain enlightenment. So he simply took his seat beneath a tree and stayed put. He vowed to stay present and let the world unfold on its own terms. He vowed to remain seated on the earth. If enlightenment dawned, so be it. If death dawned, so be it. Whatever

occurred, so be it. Siddhartha took his seat as the future Lord
Buddha and rested in the shade of a tall bodhi tree.

Eventually, by taking such a posture, he confronted his
deepest hopes and fears. His frequent guest arrived: Mara, the
Lord of Desire, this time accompanied by his tempting daughters—Tanha, Raga, and Arati—and a vast army of demons.
Mara had been tracking Siddhartha's progress toward enlightenment, tempting him, cajoling him, and dismissing his efforts. But now he could see that Siddhartha was growing near
his goal, and Mara was eager to sidetrack Siddhartha's hard
work. Clever and seductive, Mara and his daughters tried to
coax and reason with Siddhartha, arguing that he was not
prepared for enlightenment, but to no avail. Siddhartha remained still: prepared or not, so be it. Fierce and destructive,
the army of demons created hallucinations to drive him mad,
but could not. Siddhartha remained still: hallucinations or
not, so be it. Eventually Siddhartha dispatched all of Mara's
demons and conquered all of his enticements but one. As Siddhartha's enlightenment was dawning, Mara made his last
stand.

Alone now, with no armor or army hordes, Mara asked the
Buddha a simple question: "So, if you become enlightened,
who is going to say so? Who will attest to such a claim? Bring
me a witness, so that you and I can agree, and then I will
tempt you no more. So, Siddhartha, who shall be your witness?"

In response, Siddhartha made a gesture of primordial significance—a final and complete gesture that forever conquered Mara and sealed the former prince's awakening as an
enlightened Buddha: he touched the earth. He did not produce a decree from a king or queen attesting to his realization.
He did not point to a monument with his name on it. He did

ༀ། །ཐབས་མཁས་ཐུགས་རྗེ་ཤཱཀྱའི་རིགས་སུ་འཁྲུངས། །གཞན་གྱིས་མི་ཐུབ་
བདུད་ཀྱི་དཔུང་འཇོམས་པ། །གསེར་གྱི་ལྷུན་པོ་ལྟ་བུར་བརྗིད་པའི་སྐུ། །ཤཱཀྱའི་
རྒྱལ་པོའི་ཞབས་ལ་ཕྱག་འཚལ་ལོ།།

*Siddhartha Gautama, the Buddha,
in the Earth-Witnessing Mudra.*

not call on yogi friends who could recount his great acts of compassion and discipline. Siddhartha realized that no circumstances—no god, no fellow yogi, no song of praise, no monument, no decree—*nothing* could confirm or deny his fundamental sense of well-being. By touching the earth, Siddhartha finally took his seat as Lord Buddha, the fully Awakened One. By touching the earth, he proclaimed he was authentically who he was—an authenticity so fundamental, so organic, and so utterly beyond the possibility of confirmation or denial that it was destined to change history. This gesture of authenticity has been venerated for centuries in images depicting the Earth-Witnessing Mudra—the supreme symbol of well-being.

We may think that what the Buddha did is just an ancient legend, a great act achieved by an extraordinary being twenty-five hundred years ago. The posture the Buddha took beneath the bodhi tree and his expression of enlightened authenticity may, for many of us, appear to be unattainable. We could touch the earth, even roll around on it, a thousand times and still not achieve enlightenment. Achieving enlightenment, unconditional well-being, total authenticity, are for buddhas and lamas and Zen *roshis*, surely, not for ordinary people like us.

Buddhism has many names for this authenticity: *bodhichitta*, awakened heart, Zen mind, *tathagatagarbha*, awake mind, original mind, *vajra* nature. But our authenticity is not as foreign as such names seem to imply. Our ability to experience our awake mind is not as distant as a twenty-five-hundred-year-old legend. In fact, the Buddha taught that our authenticity is so immediate—so personal and intimate—that it could be experienced by all human beings by simply doing what he did beneath the bodhi tree. The Buddha pointed out that by simply being still and noticing the arising of this very moment, we would discover our awake mind, our fundamental human authenticity, on the spot.

This account of Siddhartha's awakening to his authenticity mirrors our challenge to step beyond our anxiety about work's difficulties and rediscover our natural sense of well-being and confidence. There was nothing the Buddha could point to outside himself when Mara asked him to prove his claim of enlightenment, to bring a witness to attest to his authenticity. Just so, there is nothing outside us that can offer true well-being at work—indeed, in our lives. No paycheck, no retirement fund, no promotion, and no sympathetic boss—no circumstance can give us the confidence and well-being we are seeking. Just as Mara tempted the Buddha, we too may be tempted to amass such confirmations to give us a sense of security. We may have stock options or a union pension for safekeeping. We may have credentials such as an MBA from the finest university or an impressive title such as Department Head or Executive Vice President. Or maybe we wear an imposing uniform or have our names written on signs and book covers. We may even be the president of a company, with all the accompanying prestige and entitlements. While none of these efforts are mistaken, relying on them to confirm who we are is. In the final analysis, they cannot confirm or deny who we are.

In Buddhism, recognizing this authenticity, which cannot be confirmed or denied, is a very practical matter; it is not wishful thinking. It is not something that we can make up or manufacture. A true sense of well-being is not simply a first-rate notion that we "ought" to be authentic. If that were the case, Buddhism would, in the end, be nothing but plain old idealism. Nor can we collect a true sense of authenticity by going to etiquette classes or courses in being a good citizen. Being polite and civilized is a worthy and decent pursuit, but if being authentic were simply that, a mere set of rules would suffice. In Buddhism, recognizing our authenticity is a very practical, powerful, and immediate experience.

The *Oxford English Dictionary* defines authenticity as what makes something fully and genuinely what it is. Something is authentic because it can draw on its *original authority* to make it unquestionably what it is, not a fake or imitation. If we were to purchase a Rembrandt or a thoroughbred Irish horse, for example, it would be a very practical and worthwhile matter to determine whether we were buying an authentic item. We might have an art historian examine the paint or inspect the brush strokes to see if she could recognize the original authority of the painting—that the painting originated with Rembrandt. Or we might visit the stud farm where our champion horse was reared to examine health records and pedigree papers and consider the horse's noble lineage. We would then examine our horse's conformation—the height of its withers, the thickness of its chest and girth. We might even review X rays to inspect lung capacity for endurance. We would look to see if we can recognize the original authority of the horse. We might actually discern in our horse the great champion from which she descended—an original Kentucky Derby winner.

In the same way, Buddhism considers the search for our human authenticity a practical and worthy matter, in which we experience directly the original authority from which we arise. The Buddhist path seeks to discover an origin, to determine firsthand the original authority within our very person that empowers us with unshakable well-being and gives us the confidence that we are exactly who we are, where we are, with no need of outside confirmation. In the Buddhist tradition, the primary way we inspect our pedigree and discover our authenticity is through sitting meditation, which is exactly what the Buddha did at the base of the bodhi tree.

The mindfulness meditation originally taught by the Buddha to his monks and nuns is deceptively simple. Essentially, it requires that we sit up straight, keep our eyes open, and stay present with the arising moment for as long as possible.

The rub is "for as long as possible." Invariably our minds wander and we find ourselves thinking. We could be recalling our breakfast meal, how tasty it was, the strawberries and coffee. Or we could be preparing an angry speech we intend to deliver to an ungrateful boss. Or we could be thinking of a lover or daughter or father and how much we miss and care for this person. Sitting meditation reveals many things, but first it shows us that we spend an enormous amount of time talking to ourselves and not being immediately present. We discover that we live our lives in a kind of rehearsal behind the curtain of our thoughts, rehearsing what we could have done differently and what we will do differently in the future. In the Buddhist tradition, being authentic requires that we step out of the rehearsal and engage life directly with all its uncertainties, delights, and messes. To be authentic is to stop imitating who we would like to be and touch the earth of our original authority right here, right now, fully and completely, and acknowledge who we are already.

Sitting for fifteen minutes, an hour, a day, or maybe even an entire month alternating between internal rehearsals and simply being present is an enormously boring proposition. Yet, surprisingly, it is a most useful way to make friends with ourselves and to discover our authenticity. Like hand-sanding a piece of cherry wood to prepare it for an oil finish, sitting meditation slowly and gradually refines our mind, smoothing out distractions and highlighting our original unique grain— the beauty of our natural sense of well-being. Sitting meditation is a remarkably gentle act in which we permit ourselves to simply *be*. The practice requires precision and strength and personal bravery. But such exertion resolves itself in the gentle realization that we are simply sitting—simply being. We discover that our body and mind can relax and synchronize in the lively sharpness of our senses and the present moment. We learn to drop our rehearsals—our anxieties over failure and unknown possibilities and our hopes for success and security— and for a moment to "not know" what is about to happen. For just a moment we become available to the world around us without our preconceptions and biases. We lighten up on ourselves, slow our constant rush to fix our situation, and become curious about our world rather than threatened by it. We glimpse that simply being who we are, where we are is unavoidable, genuine, and composed; we discover our pedigree, our authenticity. This discovery of authenticity through the practice of sitting meditation provides us with the core tool for developing the same composed and genuine attitude at work.

If we examine our experience of sitting meditation closely, we will discover that we are expressing something that has gone unnoticed. When we let go of our thoughts and bring our attention to the immediate moment, if we notice carefully, we will see that we *trust ourselves thoroughly*. Letting go on the cushion, at first, is a small step, like a young child learning to swim in the ocean. We let go of our rehearsals briefly and leap into the present moment, only to hesitate and rush back from the cold, tapering ocean waves, back into the seeming comfort of our inner thoughts. Over time we may trust ourselves to

wade further out into our life, staying with the present moment longer, braving the ten-foot breakers and surging sea. By
doing such a thing, by letting go of our thoughts and engaging
life directly in all of its rawness and power, we actually exhibit
a confidence in ourselves that cannot be denied or confirmed.
There are no life preservers. There are no emotional guarantees. There is no one looking over our shoulder congratulating
us for meditating well. We rely solely on our own innate abilities and resources.

Over time such trust in ourselves extends into our lives off
the cushion, where we learn to swim out past the breaking
waves and into the vast ocean of everyday life. We discover
that we can trust ourselves completely; we can be authentic
with life's circumstances, especially at work. We discover that
no stock option gods, no song of praise from a boss, no decree
of promotion, no paycheck or bonus, no new job or project,
no amount of political power—nothing can substitute for our
basic confidence in our original authority. Such confidence is
unshakable because nothing can confirm or deny it.

Being authentic at work is not particularly dramatic. It does
not require that we rush into our boss's office and finally speak
our mind, tossing our career to the wind. Nor does it require
that we finally break out and quit our job and become what
we have always wanted to be: a banjo player or quilter. Rather,
being authentic is more unassuming, a resting in our natural
sense of well-being. Such confidence permits us to become
available to our work world, to be intrigued by the entire proposition of work. As we drop our rehearsals, and our body and
mind synchronize more and more, we become present and
available to our work, interested in its details and practices.
We are not trapped by work's routines or our fears and preconceptions. We become free to engage our world fearlessly and

skillfully, learning and exploring as we go. Letting go of personal territory and relying on our innate sense of authenticity is not a particularly dramatic proposition, but it is subtle, powerful, demanding, and liberating all at the same time. "Be authentic" is a fundamental proclamation that *who we are, where we are* arises from an original authority, one that makes us decent, intelligent, and profoundly resourceful.

3

Cultivate li

WORK MAKES conflicting demands on us: compete fiercely but be cooperative, make tough decisions but be considerate, build a highly profitable business but don't cut any corners, pursue rewards but don't get greedy. Under such circumstances, finding a "moral compass" to guide our behavior—to help us be decent, fair, and honorable—can be challenging. Some of us may consider it our highest priority.

Many companies publish a code of ethical guidelines. Training programs teach us how to respect our colleagues' diverse lifestyles or how to behave ethically and lawfully when conducting business. We learn regulations and policies intended to promote a fair, respectful, and lawful work environment. We are encouraged to speak up if we feel that the code is being broken or that our work setting fosters unethical or demeaning behavior. Such efforts to promote decency at work are worthy and necessary—yet surprisingly inadequate.

In January 2003 *Time* magazine chose Cynthia Cooper, former vice president of internal audit for WorldCom; Coleen Rowley, special agent with the FBI; and Sherron Watkins, former vice president of corporate development for Enron, as Persons of the Year. They were recognized as people who most affected world events during 2002—not because they found the cure for cancer or negotiated the end to a war but, rather, in the words of *Time* magazine's editor: "They were people who did right by just doing their jobs rightly—which means ferociously, with eyes open and with the bravery the rest of us always hope we have."

The stories of these three women are actually not that remarkable. Faced with troubling difficulties at work, they took the time to examine the detail, get perspective, make hard choices, and then behave decently and truthfully. What makes their stories extraordinary is that so many others did not do the same. Rather than "doing their jobs rightly, with eyes open," hundreds of well-trained accountants bought into illegal accounting scams. Dozens of law-enforcement officers held back vital information on potential criminal activity out of fear of offending superiors. Executives from the largest companies in the world paid themselves hundreds of millions of dollars in bonuses despite their failure to conduct business properly. How is it that so many did not "do their jobs rightly"? How could it be that these three women are the exception rather than the rule?

Like these women, many of us confront instances of selfish, rude, unethical, and at times even unlawful behavior on the job. Many of us have witnessed accounting rules disregarded, conflicts of interest overlooked, and uncivil behavior toward subordinates ignored. We have seen products pilfered, frivolous lawsuits filed, and greed openly celebrated. Work, with all its creative promise and challenge, often turns self-serving and corrupt, and rule books alone can't provide the guidance needed to promote honesty and fairness on the job. The ethics courses and codes of conduct seem to be missing something. What is missing is our ability to cultivate *li*.

In ancient China around 500 BCE, thousands of burdensome social rituals dominated people's lives. When to bow, what brocade to wear, how to address a government official, what ceremony to conduct, even what ornament to rest by the fireplace, and much, much more were all dictated by a rigid social code called *li*. Through the centuries many Chinese citizens had learned to perform these rituals mechanically, turning ancient custom into worthless and often oppressive ceremony. Confucius, the great Chinese philosopher from that time, found such mindless ritual deeply damaging to Chinese society. According to Confucius, Chinese ancestors had originally shaped the rituals as a way to inspire people to be responsible toward one another and respectful of their world. But with such purpose lost, many found themselves behaving like puppets, following empty rules rather than living as dignified citizens of a great culture. In Confucius's view, the original intent of *li* had been lost, with disastrous effects.

Some historians believe the term *li* was first used by artists of ancient China who mined and cut jade, a gemstone cherished to this day throughout China. One of the enduring difficulties in carving jade into figures and decorative designs is its tendency to crack along natural contours. Some historians speculate that these lines along which the stone would gracefully and naturally crack were once called the *li* of the stone. The carver's great challenge was to incorporate this tendency to break along elegant lines into a work of art, thus producing a work of rare beauty that relied inherently on the stone's natural *li*. This original carver's skill of bringing forth the natural beauty of the jade evolved over many centuries into a collection of techniques for sawing, cutting, sanding, and polishing jade. These techniques were handed down from teacher to student over the centuries as a body of wisdom also called *li*. Eventually the term *li* came to signify any social ritual intended to reveal the natural decency and goodness of being human. So it is from these—the carver's hand, the natural elegance of jade, and Confucius's love of humanity—that we can learn to be decent by cultivating *li*.

Just as jade has a natural tendency to break along elegant lines, Confucius observed that human beings have a natural instinct to behave decently toward one another. A kind gesture, a passing smile, a desire to help others, all spontaneously arise out of a basic human goodness or tendency to be decent. According to Confucius, this tendency, *li*, was the source of all proper and decent human behavior. Cultivating a profound respect for this human goodness, he taught, is at the very heart of leading a worthy life. Just as jade cutters respect the *li* of the stone, cultivating *li* in society is central to promoting integrity and human dignity, requiring commitment and discipline. By cultivating *li*, human decency is never taken for granted but is acknowledged, respected, and preserved throughout all human activity—especially at work. Otherwise, when *li* is ignored, men and women can find themselves following pointless ritual, obeying the letter but not the spirit of accounting rules, remaining loyal out of fear, and avoiding rather than shouldering responsibility. Confucius considered a leader's central task in shaping human culture to be like that of a jade cutter: to bring forth the natural wholesomeness of humanity—to inspire and nourish *li*, thereby promoting the health, wisdom, and spiritual well-being of all citizens.

* * *

It is one thing to say that *li* is our instinct to be decent and humane, but how do we access this inner "moral compass" of integrity? Recognizing *li* within ourselves can be quite simple and straightforward. One way to acknowledge *li* is to try to deny it. For example, the next time someone extends his or her hand to you in a greeting, imagine for a moment how it would feel if you did not extend your hand in return, leaving the other person's gesture of friendship denied. Most of us would feel very uncomfortable. Try not shaking a person's extended hand and see. Or the next time you are entering a crowded store or restaurant, don't hold the door for the person exiting but simply enter first, squeeze past the person, and don't look back—just keep walking. Try it. It is almost impossible to do—it feels so improper and awkward. These small instances demonstrate the irritation of going against or corrupting *li*, the natural grain of our basic decency.

There are countless simple examples of how *li* in its utter humanness pervades our lives: giving directions to a disoriented tourist, returning a lost wallet, offering a seat to an elderly person, holding the elevator door for a colleague. Rather than being some grand philosophical notion from ancient China, *li* actually is our humanity at its most basic level—an instinct that guides us to be helpful, honorable, and gracious toward one another. No rule book can teach us to extend such respect toward our fellow humans and our world. It is our *li*, our nature, to extend such simple and noble gestures. When we fail to acknowledge and cultivate this basic decency, rudeness, violence, and selfishness become routine and decency more the exception to the rule than an everyday bond between people. Without integrity or even basic politeness toward others, we lose our respect for our world.

Cultivating *li* at work starts with extending these simple

courtesies toward our colleagues, not in the sense of being overly polite or contrived, but naturally respectful and accommodating. Over time, by cultivating such respect for others, we develop a kind of "relaxed diplomacy" that becomes part of our work style. Because we are considerate, we no longer need to apologize for being tough or straightforward; we no longer need to always make the safe decision or imagine the worst about workplace difficulties. We develop the confidence to sense when to be tactful and restrained and when to be forthcoming and direct. By cultivating *li*, ethics emerge as a natural expression of the mind free from fear and aggression, not something we learn from a rule book. As our commitment to *li* develops, so does our trust in ourselves that we will be decent, that we will "do our jobs rightly, with eyes open." We discover that our inner moral compass is made of jade and that being authentic is nothing other than following the natural contours of who we are.

How, then, do we know how to conduct ourselves in especially difficult situations, such as those faced by Cooper, Rowley, and Watkins? According to Confucius: "We know what is proper (*li*), especially in difficult situations, from the wisdom arising out of contemplation."

Confucius suggests here that it is from the stillness of contemplation, not from rule books or manuals, that we gain the confidence to make tough decisions, do what is best, and conduct ourselves skillfully. "Listening to that inner voice," "trusting a gut feeling," "reaching deep inside for the answer," or "going with what the heart says" are all common refrains that speak to this extraordinary resource of *li* that we can draw on at difficult times.

Training in the Awake at Work slogans is a contemplation practice designed for cultivating *li* at work, and other contemplation practices are suggested in the appendix "Five Contemplations for Cultivating *Li*." By regularly reflecting on our work experience with the slogans, we can learn to drop our fear and resistance and trust that our integrity and humaneness will guide us to behave decently at work. Rather than signing off on rigged financials, we can actually trust our *li* and, in Cooper's words, "feel a personal obligation" to tell the truth. Rather than watching management steal millions of dollars in undeserved bonuses, we can trust our *li* and, like Watkins, do "the hardest thing in my life" and point out that Enron's management had fallen victim to "the power of greed and the power of denial." Rather than hiding mistakes and avoiding difficulties, we can trust our *li* and, like Rowley, stop "covering up . . . only to save face." By being honest with ourselves in contemplation, we discover that Cooper, Rowley, and Watkins are not exceptions but three women who, like us, are simply decent.

"Cultivate *li*" encourages us to protect and nourish our inherent desire to behave honestly, responsibly, and respectfully. We can treat our competitors fairly even as we negotiate sharply against them. We may have to put a colleague in a tough position, but we can still be available and open and respectful. Even under tense, adversarial circumstances, we can be diplomatic and skillful while remaining deliberate, honest, and tough. Cultivating *li* reminds us that we are nobly endowed with a basic dignity and wholesomeness that can inspire and uplift not just ourselves but human society overall.

4

Work is a mess

MANY OF US COME to work with the hope that we can control our jobs. We want to be the capable authors of our work, not helpless victims of unplanned circumstance. We want to feel on top of our game and in command of the details, and we want work to stay in place so that we don't need to worry.

Yet work will not stay in place, despite all our efforts. Financial reports and spreadsheets bring the appearance of order. Routines and schedules seem reliable. Our computer systems and management abilities offer a certain kind of predictability. But what we set out wanting to do at work is never what we end up with. Work, by its very nature, is unpredictable and messy, chaotic and surprising.

Such chaos can affect us very directly and very personally. We go to work expecting one thing, and we get quite another. We may accept a new job with all its promise and challenge. Then when we get there, we find out that the manager who hired us is leaving for an opportunity elsewhere. We are left with a new boss and a different challenge altogether. Or maybe we have launched a new and promising product line—

say a game to teach children how to name countries around the world—only to discover that the packaging instructions on the one hundred thousand units are in French and we *thought* we had ordered English. Perhaps we have convinced our boss to invest in a new project; we build a team and create momentum. Then we find out midstream that the budget is cut and we must fire our newly hired staff. Such untidiness can seem to put our routines, financial security, sense of accomplishment, and much more in question.

This kind of predictable unpredictability happens every day to thousands of us. And yet we somehow end up relating to these very common circumstances as threats and disasters, losing our sense of confidence and creative challenge. Typically, we treat work's surprises as merely mistakes, missteps, or blunders that should have been otherwise, events that we should have prevented. We so much want our world to run smoothly—no uncertainties, no surprises, no uncomfortable conflicts. We want to be on top of our game, not striking out or dropping the ball. But if work's messy surprises are not just mistakes or liabilities or weaknesses, what are they? And how can we better respond to them?

The reality is that there is no solution to work's inherent chaos and messiness. Work by its very nature will always be uncertain. The good news is that work's messiness and uncertainty need not be distressing. They may, in fact, be just what we are looking for.

In the ancient Chinese text *The Art of War*, the renowned strategist-general Sun Tzu gives the following instruction:

> *When in battle,*
> *Use the orthodox to engage,*
> *Use the extraordinary to attain victory.*

While our workplace may not be a battlefield, Sun Tzu's words contain some sound advice on how to relate skillfully to work's surprises.

In this brief instruction, Sun Tzu is explaining to his warrior leaders that they should come to battle with the "orthodox" strategies in place. This means that they will have studied a wide range of tactics and disciplines. They will have devised plans ahead of time—anticipating the enemy's maneuvers and predisposition. Soldiers will have been trained in combat and weaponry, officers drilled in battlefield tactics, weapons positioned, and defenses fortified. It is from this, the orthodox, that they will *engage* battle.

But *victory*, Sun Tzu points out, does not come from such preparations. Victory is attained from the "extraordinary." Here Sun Tzu is revealing to warrior leaders a powerful reality of war: it is unpredictable and chaotic—and it is in this untidiness that the warrior general finds victory. A change in weather, an error on a battle-plan map, a weapon that discharges prematurely—all unanticipated yet inevitable—are what the warrior general remains constantly alert for and ready to exploit to his or her advantage. According to Sun Tzu, it is the infinite unshapable variations of war that offer the strategist the levers for victory.

How the warrior leader remains ever alert for the extraordinary is of the utmost importance to Sun Tzu. We cannot sit at the edge of our seats waiting to pounce on surprises like a cat on a mouse. Being greedy for success or victory is not the point. Rather, Sun Tzu stresses throughout *The Art of War* that the warrior leader must possess victory in the very fiber of his or her being from the very start, before the battle even begins. Sun Tzu teaches that the warrior leader must be relaxed and open to the present moment at all times. The more at ease the warrior is with the situation at hand, the more open and powerful and fearless he or she becomes as a leader. Sun Tzu's instruction on engaging the extraordinary is to first "know oneself" and, through that knowing, to work directly with conflict, appreciate the immediate moment, and let natural intelligence arise. In short, be awake!

Sun Tzu's use of the orthodox and the extraordinary can be applied to our experience at work. We use routines such as our business plans, financial forecasts, staff meetings, and monthly reports to *engage* our work. We train ourselves with MBAs and CPAs—the orthodox. But according to Sun Tzu, we will never succeed at work if we rely exclusively on such things. Only by remaining alert and open to the extraordinary events—the untidy and unpredictable—and engaging them directly and openly can we truly succeed.

A talented employee recruited by a competitor becomes an opportunity to promote new talent from within—and have a friend within the "competitor's camp." The economy slumps, our profitability is down—but so is our competitor's, who now is ripe for acquisition. Accusations of unfair work practices provide an opportunity to refresh policies top to bottom. A lack of new product ideas becomes just the chance to reach down into the lower ranks and listen to the unheard potential innovators. The conflicts and difficulties at work hold the possibility of success if we are open enough to engage them without resentment or fear.

If we were to adapt Sun Tzu for the workplace, we might translate his three-line instruction a bit differently:

> *When at work,*
> *Use established routines to pursue objectives,*
> *Use messiness and surprises to innovate and succeed.*

"Work is a mess" encourages us to first recognize that we can never have a completely neat relationship with our livelihood. Treating work's messiness as if it were a mistake or liability only creates further unnecessary distress and resentment. By developing the attitude that work is a mess, we can learn to relax and be curious about the surprises and interruptions. By engaging the messiness of work directly—appreciating both the advantages and disadvantages—we become fully equipped to engage such events in all their variations. We have the ingenuity, good humor, and curiosity to adapt and innovate—to be victorious, no matter what the circumstances.

PART TWO

DEVELOPING A
COMPOSED ATTITUDE

The eleven slogans in this section question some of our most fundamental habits and preconceptions about why and how we work, and invite us to engage our jobs with an entirely different attitude.

- No ground, no guarantees, just *now*
- A bucket and a thumb
- Your present job is going away
- Step beyond the silence of fear
- Power is unnerving
- Be cynical
- Contemplate wealth
- At times of risk and stress, cultivate stillness
- Cultivate "kitchen sink" mentality
- Be kind to yourself
- Open

When we mix these slogans with our daily work, we come face-to-face with the reality that nothing is guaranteed in life and that our search for security at work is pointless. By being utterly candid with ourselves about our motives at work, we begin to develop a natural composure that is neither seeking confirmation nor fearful of work's unknowns. We acknowledge our basic resourcefulness, learn to trust and care for ourselves, and express an open and realistic attitude toward our jobs and our colleagues. The eleven slogans of this section point to the delightful and shocking reality that anything can and does happen at work, and we have no option but to be open as circumstances unfold.

5

No ground, no guarantees, just now

To be awake at work is not a fixed or tidy state of mind that we achieve at some point, a point at which we have finally made it and are once and for all awake. There is no final accomplishment we can look to, no state of mind that we can give a bonus to or promote to CEO. Rather, being awake at work is engaging our work precisely, genuinely, and directly as it constantly unfolds, moment by moment, without bias or pretense. One moment the phone is silent, the next it is ringing. Today we have a job; our routines and responsibilities are laid out before us. The next day our job is gone—no routines, no responsibilities. Now we make the sale, now we lose the sale. To be awake at work is to engage each circumstance now, on its own vivid, fluid, and uncertain terms.

When we wakefully engage each moment for what it is, we notice that who we are is put into question all the time. Just as our work circumstances change and shift, so do we. Who we are and who we would like to become are as uncertain as the circumstances we face. Try as we may, we cannot find a solid identity at work. Today we are a supportive and helpful colleague; tomorrow someone considers us problematic. Our new title of Vice President is one moment exhilarating, the next burdensome, and other times irrelevant. Today we may be a successful executive, a team leader, or a deal maker. Tomorrow we are jobless, no longer established but undefined and searching. To be awake at work is to acknowledge that the entire situation—our job and our version of ourselves at work—is fluid and constantly changing. In short: no ground, no guarantees, just *now*.

Of course, we could consider such a viewpoint ridiculous. Our jobs are not *that* uncertain and groundless. We know who we are and we know what our jobs are—no question, no real doubt. Circumstances may change and difficulties may arise, but we adapt—we "soldier on," as the British say. And to a great degree, most of us do just that, doing the best we can. Being awake at work does not entirely question such conviction. We work hard to have some predictability in our lives, which is a decent and worthy aim. But by being awake at work, we also permit work's uncertainties to manifest as fully and vividly as they naturally occur, moment by moment. We are willing to feel all the textures of work's risks and difficulties without the painful defenses of resentment or arrogance or fear. We do not need to water down the fact that there are no guarantees. Nor do we need to sugarcoat hard business facts, dress up results to make them more than they are, or pretend that the "emperor has new clothes" when we know otherwise. To be awake at work is to be thoroughly aware that anything can and does happen at work and to have no need to pretend otherwise.

Typically, business treats groundlessness or uncertainty as a liability or inconvenience, a temporary mirage on our way to perfect and lasting control. It's as if work perfectly executed would eliminate uncertainty, guaranteeing success with no surprises, no mistakes, no risks misjudged. To be awake at work is to take exactly the opposite viewpoint. Rather than being a liability to be eliminated, groundlessness is acknowledged as the foundation or essential nature of all that we experience— *the* basic and unavoidable fact of life. The reality that everything is constantly changing provokes and tickles our attention because we never really know what's going to happen next. We are awake at work precisely because everything is in question. Everything we are, everything we do, everything we want and desire, is basically in question each and every moment. This powerful and sharp reality demands that we *wake up*.

Some of us may say: "Since there is no ground and there are no guarantees, and I don't know what's about to happen, I can relax, kick back, have another cup of coffee, and wait and see." The French saying *"C'est la vie!"* becomes our slogan: "That's life. Sometimes things work out, other times things don't go so well. No need to get too involved. *C'est la vie!*" Such an approach treats our experience of uncertainty as an excuse to abandon the penetrating vividness of our immediate experience. The demanding reality of "No ground, no guarantees, just *now*" becomes our reason to take another nap. We shrug our shoulders and give in to a kind of depression because we can't control our world. We light up another cigarette, put on dark glasses, and watch the immediate moment unfold through a smoky haze.

But groundlessness is not an excuse for taking a nap or hand-wringing. It is instead a sharp invitation to "Wake up— pay attention—appreciate the world around you!" Groundlessness becomes the landscape that informs, unsettles, and awakens who we are and everything we do. Whoever we are, a world-famous doctor or the local car mechanic, we know our status is fleeting. Whether we are repairing a broken heart valve or a worn transmission, we know that fundamentally we do not know what will happen next.

When we acknowledge that there is no ground, no guarantee, just *now*, we become pioneers: this very moment, right here and now, becomes unfamiliar territory to be explored. Our routines may be familiar and what is expected of us may be distinct and concrete, but there is always—*always*—something new and unknown happening. "No ground, no guarantees, just *now*" reminds us to become pioneers of the immediate moment in everything we do at work. As pioneers we do not need to weigh ourselves down with a collection of fixed views and habits; we can travel light, retaining what is useful and letting go of whatever becomes ineffective. As pioneers we become seasoned travelers who are well aware that anything can and does happen. A storm could blow in any moment or our company could be bought by a competitor. Just around the corner we may find a mountain spring where we can refresh ourselves or a new product idea that could reinvigorate our marketing strategy. As pioneers we are alert and prepared because there is always, *always* something new and surprising.

Most important, "No ground, no guarantees, just *now*" reminds us that we are free. By acknowledging that who we are and what we do at work is never fixed, we discover a basic freedom, because anything can happen next. Remaining open to a world that is so vastly unpredictable requires us to be exceedingly brave and to trust that we are fully equipped to engage such events. To be that free is to be utterly available to our lives—to trust that we have the ingenuity, good humor, and curiosity to adapt and thrive, no matter what the circumstances.

6

A bucket and a thumb

WHEN WE ARE SUCCESSFUL at work, many people rely on us. The decisions we make each day have a serious impact on others; we become, for them, essential to "getting the job done." Making such an important contribution can happen from behind the CEO's desk or from behind a cash register. We may set prices for a rare and much-needed health product, or maybe we have the simple yet extraordinary talent of fixing any appliance. All of us, in our own way, play an important role at work, and we can come to see ourselves as indispensable.

Feeling indispensable at work can quietly creep up on us, creating a potentially disastrous blind spot. Because we are relied on and we have a proven track record, we can slowly begin to feel a false sense of confidence, certain that our managing and handling of problems is unquestionable. Because we feel so confident, we end up ignoring advice from our colleagues and signals from our work environment. We are so busy being indispensable that we find ourselves overlooking the obvious and, possibly, terribly out of touch with our jobs.

59

I once learned the hard lesson of feeling indispensable through the eyes of a publishing colleague, Bailey. Bailey had built a very profitable publishing business, so successful that it was acquired by the company that employed me. He was considered a leader in the industry and sat on many publishing committees. He gave public addresses at conferences and book expos. Hundreds of employees reported to Bailey, and he was widely admired, though considered a bit stodgy and fixed in his ways. He was skeptical of new technology and slow to consider new ways to organize and produce books. Bailey tolerated rather than valued his new corporate partner and, in his new role as division president, often ignored corporate priorities that required his attention.

My job was to renegotiate Bailey's employment contract, which was coming up for renewal in six months. No one in management wanted to lose Bailey, and he knew it. He ran a tight ship, and we did not want to compete against him if he were to leave the company and join a competitor. He clearly felt he held all the cards.

For the most part, our negotiations went well. We resolved most issues except one, which was keeping me up at night: Bailey refused to report to his new boss as part of the contract. He had been unhappy and increasingly frustrated since his company was acquired, and it appeared that he intended to bring his frustrations to a head. He wanted his boss out of the way and felt he had the power to make it happen.

I was curious about how Bailey's boss, Rachel, was going to handle this demand. It was obviously a delicate issue, and I was not sure how to present the problem. I kept rehearsing what I was going to say, and in my mind the conversation sounded more and more like a kind of joke: "So, how are the contract negotiations going with Bailey?" I would imagine her asking me. "Well, the good news is that he wants to stay, but the bad news is that he's thinking that maybe instead of him reporting to you, you could mow his lawn or do his gardening," would be my reply.

When the time came to discuss the issue with Rachel, she quickly took charge of the conversation. "So, how's the dialogue going with Bailey?" she asked. "Pretty good, except for one real difficult point," I replied with a grimace. "Oh, it's the 'I'm too good to report to her and since I am indispensable, could someone do something about her' clause," Rachel responded with a laugh. "It's just a bucket and a thumb, Michael—just a bucket and a thumb."

"A bucket and a thumb?" I asked. "What's that supposed to mean?" Rachel sat back and explained: "Bailey suffers from thinking he's indispensable. The fact is, no matter how indispensable you think you are, when you leave a job, the impact is the same as when you take your thumb out of a bucket of water: practically none. This company would do just fine without Bailey. We have hundreds of hardworking people, and they will continue with or without him. No one is indispensable, not even Bailey. And if, like Bailey, you think you are *that* indispensable, there's a much bigger problem to be fixed."

Needless to say, Bailey was fired about thirty days later and Rachel went on to manage the business without him. Her insights into Bailey's blind spot left a lasting impression on me. She had seen that Bailey's sense of indispensability had rendered him unable to adapt and manage the difficulties of change. Bailey had become used to the way he did things, and his business "eyes and ears" had become closed. Rigidly attached to the status quo, he was unwilling to accept new ways of doing business, such as considering the impending impact of technology and coordinating investment decisions with sister divisions. His resistance to his new boss and his new corporate owners was, in reality, his fear of having to manage the marketplace complexities that were fast closing in on his business.

He was, however, willing to threaten to leave if he did not get his way, to hold the entire company hostage. Bailey came first—over his boss this time, but who or what was going to be next? Maybe next month corporate profit goals would not be to his liking, or maybe he would refuse to commit corporate dollars to new authors and projects. Bailey's overconfidence was going to derail him and his division sooner or later, and Rachel decided, quite correctly, that sooner was better than later.

The slogan "A bucket and a thumb" reminds us to beware of a false sense of confidence. No matter how capable we may be at work, the humbling reality is that we are all replaceable. Success need not lead us to complacency or smugness. By reminding ourselves that our work world would move on quite nicely without us, we can adopt a balanced attitude, enjoying our own accomplishments and taking a simple pride in helping others to succeed as well.

7

Your present job is going away

WE ALL WANT to keep our jobs. Our income pays for our children's education. Our health insurance keeps us and our loved ones safe and healthy. Our savings give us something to rely on for the future. We all want some stability in our lives: a predictable paycheck, a place of employment, familiar colleagues. The logic is quite simple: if we do our jobs well, we will be rewarded, we will have a job, and our lives will be somewhat secure.

The problem is, the logic doesn't hold up. For an infinite number of reasons, people lose their jobs every day. More than one thousand Americans lose their job every hour—many if not most of whom were doing their job quite well. The reality is that no matter how talented we are or how well we perform at work, no matter how loyal or dedicated we have been, we can find ourselves without a job, sometimes without warning—and we know it.

The prospect of losing our job is distressing. Even contemplating the possibility makes us feel groundless and unsettled, because so much seems to be at risk: our financial security, reputation, safety, sense of self-worth, and even our identity. In our candid moments, we know our jobs are not secure or permanent. Many of us see our colleagues losing their jobs or we read daily newspaper reports about new rounds of layoffs, high unemployment, and tough economic times around the world. We know the score. We know that circumstances may arise that could put our livelihood at risk.

If we examine our discomfort more closely, however, we may notice that having no guarantees is not the root cause of our distress. We feel anxious not because of the reality of uncertainty but because we continually struggle against it, pretending that things are not so precarious. We are anxious because we persist in a futile search for the impossible, expecting our jobs to provide security in an uncertain and constantly changing world. At the heart of our uneasiness is a frustration with ourselves that we keep trying to guarantee our lives when we know that it is impossible.

In the face of company-wide layoffs, department reorganizations, discontinued projects, accounts lost to competitors, we find ourselves clinging to the *appearance* of security. We may ignore certain unpleasant details or complain about "unfair criticism." When we feel threatened, we may be quick to place blame or seek assurances that things will be okay. Insisting that work provide security means that we sometimes find ourselves spending more time and effort *holding on* to our jobs than actually performing them.

"Your present job is going away" reminds us that we can stop expecting security and guarantees from work. We can drop the struggle to hold on. We can be honest with ourselves about what our jobs can and cannot do for our lives. Much at work is unruly, unreasonable, at times unfair, and never, ever secure. While this may be an unpleasant fact, it does not require us to struggle or deceive ourselves. The facts may be stark, but we need not be afraid of them.

Of course, "Your present job is going away" is not suggesting that we should be thoughtless or that we should not seek predictable work. But we need to be utterly realistic in our endeavors. No job is permanent, no income secure; no career path does not, on occasion, take a strange and difficult turn. Our job can neither rescue us from life's uncertainties nor secure our reputation, identity, or self-worth.

By being realistic about what work can and cannot provide us, we can begin to relate with our job properly and precisely and not as a matter of survival. Rather than holding on to our job for security and stability, we can let go and trust ourselves. We are resourceful. We can engage work confidently and authentically. We have the courage to engage work on its own terms rather than trying to find false security. Creative challenges are simply what they are: challenges, not a matter of survival. Workplace difficulties are exactly what they are: difficulties, not a matter of impending disaster. Contributing to our world—making a new product, providing a reliable service, helping those in need—is a brisk and forward-looking venture demanding that we be confident and resourceful, not haunted by hopes for security and fear of disaster.

By contemplating the reminder "Your present job is going away," we are deliberately rearranging how we think about work in order to be realistic. The effort we spend worrying about holding on to our jobs can be freed up and applied to living our lives courageously. Just like everything else in life, our jobs are not permanent, and there is nothing to hold on to, which might actually be good news.

8

Step beyond the silence of fear

In April 2003 senior management at the *New York Times* discovered that one of their reporters, Jayson Blair, was consistently lying when reporting the news. Typically, businesses treat egregious behavior such as fraud, theft, sexual harassment, or in this case, misrepresenting the news as the *occasional* severe personnel problem that requires swift action: fire the culprit and get back to work. Unfortunately, such behavior is often a symptom of a greater problem, and this was apparently the case at the *New York Times*. While the executive editor of the paper, Howell Raines, may originally have hoped simply to fire Blair, learn a quick lesson, and get on with business, the staff at the *Times* felt otherwise. In reaction to the scandal, newsroom employees, reporters, editors, and staff throughout the paper expressed angry complaints not about Jayson Blair but about feeling "bullied," "poorly led," "ignored," and generally disrespected. For many at the *Times*, Blair was not a passing problem but a window into a deeply troubled workplace where "a sense of decency was either taken for granted or lost in the rush to pursue news." At the heart of the troubles was a very simple and painful reality expressed starkly by the executive editor himself: "Fear is a problem to such an extent, I was told, that editors are scared to bring me bad news."

What Howell Raines discovered in firing Jayson Blair was the silent and deadly effect fear has on business. In the end the scandal cost Mr. Raines and some of his senior managers their jobs, but the impact was far greater than a few people being fired. What became painfully clear when the dust settled at the *Times* was that an entire institution known worldwide for honesty and accuracy in reporting was, in fact, an organization that could not be honest with itself. A culture of fear had put into question everything that was valued and respected about the *New York Times*.

Of course, there are many examples of fear overcoming organizations: EF Hutton, Arthur Andersen, Enron, WorldCom—even the Catholic Church. Most of us have been afraid at work at some point: afraid to lose our job, afraid of being criticized or embarrassed, afraid of being disliked, afraid of confronting an uncomfortable difficulty.

We usually keep our fears to ourselves. We are not going to tell the executive editor that we feel he is a bully or say to our colleagues at a meeting, "Hey, I think I screwed up the system conversion." We may even pretend otherwise, acting tough and unapproachable rather than confused or hurt. Generally, just as at the *New York Times*, workplace fear remains in the background, staying hidden and avoided, until something breaks.

Being awake at work, on the other hand, requires that we carefully examine our fears right here, right now. The supervisor who hesitates to share an idea with an insecure boss, the secretary who is troubled by a colleague's light but sexually suggestive remarks, the board member who rubber-stamps disturbingly generous bonus payments to undeserving executives, the sales rep who is pressured to move product that she knows lacks quality—appreciating the fear behind these common workplace circumstances is central to being authentic at work. To do so, we must first understand fear's most unmistakable feature: *silence*.

Ordinarily silence brings to mind a peaceful setting or a quiet moment where we are free from the speed and clamor of life's demands. But the silence of workplace fear is not peaceful or quiet. It is the tense, unspoken anxiety of people unwilling to say what is really on their minds. By simply acknowledging the pain of such awkwardness, we take our first step beyond the silence of fear.

Of course, to step beyond the silence of fear is not just to speak our minds whenever and to whomever we please. Offering opinions at the right time and in the correct setting is central to cultivating *li* and being effective at work. In order to step beyond the silence of fear, we must first simply witness how silence conceals fear at work. When the assistant who is rudely dismissed by his boss in a meeting becomes sullen and withdrawn, we see the silence of fear. When the accountant keeps her eyes down as the sales manager presents highly questionable sales numbers to the CEO, we again see such silence. The fuming medical intern, the embarrassed waitress, the roomful of operations clerks with arms folded—by noticing such hesitation in others and examining our own reluctance to speak our mind, we heighten our awareness of workplace fear and set the stage for understanding the real difference between being cowardly and being fearless at work.

Being cowardly is to live our lives in a gnawing, uneasy state of hope and fear—fearing what might go wrong with our jobs and hoping to be safe and successful. Rather than trusting ourselves and being authentic, we view work as a basic threat that must be "handled" in order to avoid being embarrassed. We keep our fearful thoughts to ourselves and accept the status quo, no matter how dysfunctional, rather than speak our minds, which could possibly invite the worst. Our instincts to be decent and authentic conflict with our anxious desire to be safe, and we stress out and silently freeze up in order to protect our career, paycheck, reputation, or job. Such cowardice is shallow and pathetic and never achieves its goal in the end.

Being fearless, on the other hand, is to live with no guarantees. Things not only *might* go wrong at work, they will—but we trust ourselves to do our best. Rather than relating to work's messiness and difficulties as a threat, we engage them from a basic stance of confidence: that being who we are where we are is powerful and sufficient. We admit that being authentic is our only option and that hiding out in the silence of fear is fundamentally pointless.

Behaving cowardly at work is not something to be ashamed of, however. To step beyond the silence of fear, we need to admit that there is something in our lives to step beyond, namely, that we are afraid. By admitting our cowardice, we express the very courage we are seeking. When Howell Raines at the *New York Times* met with his employees days before he resigned, he attempted to confront his cowardice, admitting, "I was guilty of a failure of vigilance" and "You view me as inaccessible and arrogant" and "I am here to listen to your anger." Despite his actions being too little too late, Raines nonetheless sought to acknowledge the reality of fear and to model the possibility of courage. As a leader, he engaged his people in what was described as "an unusually raw, emotional, and candid session" where he faced work's messiness and took an important step beyond his own "hard-charging" style of cowardice.

"Step beyond the silence of fear" encourages us to be highly attuned to how denial masks fear with silence. Particularly if we are in a leadership role, we can speak skillfully with others about our fears and apprehensions and listen intently to others speak about their sensitive issues. When we hear "I could be fired for saying that!" or "We'll get in trouble for that," we should listen carefully and witness from the heart. Recognizing such awkwardness in others and ourselves is central to being fearless at work.

Stepping beyond the silence of fear requires, too, that we be attentive to how we conduct ourselves, alert to any mixed messages we may send that could confuse or upset others. Accepting criticism, listening deeply, collaborating with others, respecting privacy, discussing difficult topics thoughtfully, and being precise in our speech—all are part of how we skillfully and consistently build a workplace free from fear. To step beyond the silence of fear is to deeply appreciate the suffering many of us experience each day in getting our jobs done and to admit that all of us are worthy to be free from anxiety and fear at work.

9

Power is unnerving

POWER CAN MAKE us feel uneasy. Even hearing or saying the word can make us feel on edge. If we were to say in a meeting with our colleagues, "I want power," people would most likely feel distressed or think we were a little crazy. It just wouldn't sound right. Power isn't spoken about so offhandedly. Or if a colleague were to whisper to us, "Hey, want to see something cool here in my briefcase?" and we were to take a peek and find a million dollars in cash neatly stacked, we would probably become rather nervous. He shouldn't carry such concentrated power around in a briefcase like that. Chances are he might leave it in a taxicab.

Sometimes we are so uneasy with power we become paralyzed. Maybe a famous movie star or basketball player happens to get onto an elevator with us and we freeze up. We try to "act casual." Or we find we can barely move our lips to ask if we could have a small thread of the person's clothing for our fan club collection.

Proximity to power, our own or others', makes us feel uneasy because we intuitively sense that something may be said or done that could change our life in unknown ways. We sense possibilities but are unsure. This uncertainty makes us uneasy, yet it strongly engages us at the same time.

On the one hand, we can be attracted to such unknowns. *Maybe* our movie star will turn and say hello or *maybe* our boss is considering us for a promotion. Such "maybes" are exciting; they get our attention. On the other hand, power with all its unknowns can be frightening. Maybe we are promoted to manage a new "cutting-edge" project, only to find out that the chairman of the company considers the entire effort questionable and probably a poor investment. *Maybe* our new project is a losing proposition and our team members' hard work and careers are at risk. *Maybe* we are planning clinical trials for a new anticancer drug that has fantastic promise, but we will have to reject applications from some ailing patients, whose very lives we hold in our hands. Such "maybes" are distressing; they get our attention too.

The uncertainties of power can make us yearn for simplicity. Sometimes we long to go back to our childhood, when our parents had all the power and we didn't have to worry about life's unknowns. Or we want to be like Judge Judy—how comfortable it would be to have someone say "all rise" when we stride into the room. On the *Judge Judy Show*, we know who has the power and when decisions are going to be made. We wish power and authority could be managed in some way so life could be simple, with no surprises showing up in an elevator or a briefcase or at our desk.

However, power at work, like everything else, is complex, fluid, and unruly. Power never stays in one place but is constantly shifting and morphing. One minute our client has all the power to sign the contract. Once signed, the power shifts and *we* are the general contractor responsible for building the new $350 million city center. One minute our colleague is making the sales pitch, and the next our customer turns to us and says, "What do you think?" Power shifts from person to person; where power is concerned, there are no scripts. What we say or do on the spot can have far-reaching consequences. How we conduct ourselves—making commitments, speaking up, remaining silent, taking risks—can put into play irreversible actions that we and others will have to live with.

Power requires us to engage work *as it unfolds*—straightforwardly and without hesitation. It leaves no room for complaints, excuses, rehearsals, or blind impulse. It requires us to be fluid and resourceful, presenting ideas accurately, promoting trust, listening well, sharing authority, compromising, persuading, and much more. In short, power demands confidence. And odd as it may seem, our uneasiness with power is the key to discovering such confidence within ourselves.

If we examine our uneasiness with power closely, we will discover that it is not an inconvenience or weakness but a physical impulse to be mindful on the spot. Our body is telling us—even when we simply hear the word *power*—that there are risks at hand and we need to be alert, precise, and resourceful. Being mindful of our nervousness, rather than startled by it, puts us on our toes. We know instinctively that power demands our attention to the immediate moment. Our heart might be racing, or our mouth may become dry, or maybe our breathing begins to speed up. But we need not be shaken by this edginess. This unease is the sharp edge of our own fresh intelligence, waking us up. By slowing down mindfully, taking a deep breath and simply being present, we will discover on the spot the very confidence we are seeking.

"Power is unnerving" encourages us to be attentive to our uneasiness with authority, whether our own or that of others.

By bringing our mindfulness to this discomfort, we discover that we are naturally alert *already*—unsettled, perhaps, yet sharply prepared and attentive.

"Power is unnerving" suggests that such nervousness can become our best friend. We do not need to rehearse what we are going to say or do. We simply take a deep breath and relax into the sharpness of our uneasiness. From this place of edgy clarity, we can learn to postpone our impulse to relieve our nervousness. We can learn to restrain our haste to be comfortable. Instead, we allow ourselves to stay uncertain and rely on our natural sense of timing and openness to guide us as the situation unfolds. Maybe the person interviewing us for a job seems distracted and uninterested; rather than being disturbed by the distractions, we remain mindful. Instinctively we ask for a glass of water, and a human moment unfolds. On our sales call, we are kept waiting in the lobby: rather than rehearsing our presentation once again in our mind, we relax into our edginess and mindfully enjoy the small boredom of the moment—ordinary, simple, and fresh. If we were to meet someone as powerful as the president of the United States, we wouldn't rush to make small talk, but we could actually relax mindfully into our nervousness and suddenly discover that she has a question to ask us.

"Power is unnerving" encourages us to be suspicious if we are too comfortable with our own power. We may have the authority to write traffic tickets or drug prescriptions, declare bankruptcy or war, sign a paycheck or a billion-dollar contract, but in each instance we should be a bit unnerved by our own authority. My Buddhist teacher, Chögyam Trungpa Rinpoche, was renowned for keeping himself and his students on just such an edge. He went so far as to design a sharp point in the back of his teaching chair to remind him or anyone who took such a seat that there is no room for leaning back and relaxing when teaching Buddhism. From his point of view, nervousness was a good friend that we should listen to and respect. Whether we are dispensing power or being directed by it, we should permit our nervousness to alert us, keeping us fresh and in tune with our responsibilities.

In the end, "Power is unnerving" encourages us to make friends with our nervousness at work, to be intensely mindful of when and how we feel uneasy. For it is here, from just such edginess, that we discover that we can trust ourselves to be confident, resourceful, and precise in the immediate moment.

10

Be cynical

NORMALLY, IF WE describe ourselves as cynical, we mean that we are singularly suspicious of *other people*—skilled in recognizing hypocrisy and selfish motives. Millionaire CEOs bankrupting companies, politicians calling for ethics in the boardroom, executives granting themselves millions of stock options—the list would be long and the targets easy. As cynics, we smile wryly to ourselves with an "I told you so" written discreetly across our face, not fooled by other people's predictable charades. Ironically, if we were to look back in history, we would find the original cynics did not share such smugness. They were fiercely suspicious, to be sure—but primarily of *themselves*, not others.

The Cynic philosophers of ancient Greece taught that to find contentment in life, we need not look any further than ourselves. They considered prestige, political power, material wealth, and beauty false enticements to trust in external pleasures rather than themselves for contentment. As ascetics, Cynics became notorious for ruthlessly unmasking their own hidden desires for material "happiness." Many Cynics exposed themselves purposefully to severe criticism from their teachers and lived lives of utmost simplicity—often to the extreme. Students engaged in rude debates, taunting each other and testing each other's commitment to rejecting the corruption of worldly pleasures. And of course, they parodied Greek society at large—often in brilliant and hilarious street theater. While the Cynics were greatly admired by many in ancient Greece, they were also seen as a bit wild and a social pain in the neck. Their sarcastic street theater won them the label of *kynikos*, or "resembling dogs"—the "Cynics." But despite their biting social criticism, the Cynics were fiercely honest first about *not kidding themselves*—examining their own motives, not just those of others.

Taking a cue from the original Cynics, then, to be cynical is to first question ourselves, not others. Rather than smugly cataloging other people's hypocrisy, we permit the sharp intelligence of cynicism to become our moral compass for being honest with ourselves. The reminder encourages us to first feel our insecurities about work. Our aspirations for such things as recognition from the boss, increased authority, or a promotion to a senior position are valid, of course. We all want to succeed at work. To be cynical, however, is to look for any desire to mislead ourselves about such aspirations. How much are we invested in being validated by our boss? What do we hope to get out of such recognition? How well do we handle our authority? Do we make others comfortable, or are we arrogant and aloof? Will we be embarrassed if we are passed over for promotion? Why? By accurately sorting through our hopes and fears about success at work, we begin gradually cutting through the false enticements we attribute to our jobs and careers. Like the Cynics of old, we slowly learn to look no further than ourselves for our sense of identity or personal self-worth. We learn to rely on our inherent authenticity, our humor, open heart, and precise mind, for fulfillment and meaning in our lives.

Over time our healthy cynicism grows sharp and reliable, an intelligence that seeks no confirmation and is clear seeing, realistic, and fearless. We become accustomed to work's uncertainties and discerning toward its enticements: the well-staged presentation for a temperamental boss, a sales pitch perfectly executed to seduce the customer's "sweet spot," an accounting report seamlessly written to highlight the smiles and tone down the wrinkles, a recruiting pitch that weaves an idyllic yet one-sided picture of future employment. Rather than buying the false assurances and sugarcoated promises, we simply look closer and consider the substance over the superficial, an activity that is demanding yet inherently decent. Being cynical in such circumstances requires tough intelligence, a clear and present mind, and a steadfast character not easily seduced by external gratification.

By being cynical, we might see how others may hope to manipulate us on occasion. Since we are not easily fooled by ourselves, we are not easily fooled by others. Being wary in such a sharp way does not require us to be scornful or detached, just willing to be vigilant and candid with ourselves. We can be brutally honest with ourselves without brutalizing the world around us.

At the heart of being cynical is the sobering reminder that no promotion, bonus, paycheck, retirement fund, job perk— no lucrative contract, prestigious connection, "slap on the back," or job title—can bring us lasting satisfaction. We can stop wishing for the lottery to save us from work and be honest with ourselves. Sugarcoating, false guarantees, and momentary pleasures can never substitute for the ease of simply being who we are, where we are. The sharp candor of cynicism leaves no room for mortgaging our authenticity out of insecurity or indulgence. To be cynical, in this sense, is a noble gesture of honesty and an act of personal courage.

11

Contemplate wealth

WHAT IF ALL your money and wealth were gone in an instant? It happens every day to thousands of people around the world, so contemplating such a possibility is not that far-fetched. Imagine for a moment that you are without a job and penniless: What would you do? How would you feel? Would you see the world as hostile or helpful? If you had to live on the street, becoming invisible to people passing by, how would you deal with that? If you have a family, they would probably be destitute too. Would such a thing destroy you or deepen your wisdom?

Being penniless and unable to meet our responsibilities is something we would not wish for anybody. But by contemplating wealth in such a way—imagining ourselves suddenly and totally without it, exposed to life directly, without wealth's protection or guarantees—we can gain insight into our fears about making a living.

When contemplating wealth, consider how much seems to depend on having money. With money we can make many choices: own a home, take a vacation, retire early, and afford the best doctors and schools. Without it, so much seems at risk: the roof over our head, our family's welfare, our health, even our ability to put food on the table. Money seems to touch a deep and powerful chord within us: our passion to survive. But if our wealth were to disappear, would circumstances overwhelm us, or would we be resourceful? What would happen if we had lots of money; would we have command of our life? Is who we are that different with or without money? Contemplating wealth encourages us to consider these possibilities.

"Contemplate wealth" invites us to explore all the stories we tell ourselves about money, to examine our "money neuroses." Maybe we have money and are afraid of losing it; maybe we have lost our money and desperately want it back. Maybe we need money and worry about getting more of it, or we pretend to have money because we think and hope money's coming very soon. Maybe we have a lot of money and we notice that everyone else wants some, or maybe we feel guilty because our children have become spoiled by it. By feeling the texture of our money story lines—the physical anxiety, the haunting unease, the freedom, possibly even the claustrophobia of it all—we begin being candid with ourselves about our grasping or our embarrassment about money.

By contemplating wealth, we can feel both sides of money: it weighs us down and frees us up; it entices us yet at times upsets us; it helps us get things done and also gets in the way. Wealth's ironies come into focus: the more we need, the less there is; the more we have, the more we want. Some of us seem to work a lot and make little money; others seem to work little and make a lot of money. By contemplating wealth in such a way, we explore money as one of life's paradoxes, opening to a broader view of the fickle and unpredictable nature of money and material wealth.

On occasion when contemplating wealth, we may want to consider the world around us. The divorcing celebrities fighting over how to split up $120 million; the forty-eight thousand children who starved to death today and have every day for decades; the trillions of dollars spent on militaries around the world; the elderly neighbor who always helps out a panhandler with a dime or two; the robberies and murders; the charities and the needy. When we expand our view of wealth in this way, wealth is no longer just a personal concern but a way to understand the world around us.

Contemplating wealth encourages us to question our very understanding of wealth itself. Is there really anything outside ourselves that can offer us lasting peace or security in this ever-changing world? Can money and material wealth *really* give us confidence and joy? We need money for basic necessities, certainly, but no amount of money can relieve, for example, the suffering of our child struggling to survive leukemia. No amount of wealth can slow our parents' aging or return our lost youth. Money cannot make us a better artist or friend; nor can it make the breeze any cooler or the sky any bluer.

Or maybe wealth is a larger proposition altogether. During a conference entitled "Wealth and Authenticity," a participant defined wealth as having an abundance of what means most to you. When we contemplate wealth from this perspective, we discover we are considering a most profound issue indeed: our personal sense of well-being. Can we rediscover our original wealth, our weal: the natural sense of authenticity and prosperity that is ours simply because we are alive? Can we be alive in this uncertain and demanding world and feel at our ease—capable, confident, and cheerful? If we cut to the core of contemplating wealth, we have to ask ourselves a very basic question: Can we feel at home in our lives?

Developing a sane relationship with wealth and money is a primary challenge of work. We work in order to accomplish many things, but getting paid—the paycheck, the bonus, accounts receivable, the fee, having money, building material wealth—is central. There are some easy answers, of course, when dealing with money: be precise and careful, balance your checkbook, pay your bills on time, don't steal or cheat, pay your taxes, help others when you can. But the powerful and tough questions that money and wealth present are more important—and contemplating wealth invites us to consider them. How do we feel about money? Threatened, embarrassed, comfortable, haunted, anxious? What are these feelings trying to tell us? Are we resourceful enough to engage life with less money than we have now? Would we feel less at home in our lives?

Reflecting on our relationship to money and wealth is obviously a very personal issue and requires a commitment to asking ourselves powerful questions. Such an investigation need not be humorless and heavy-handed, however. In the appendix entitled "Contemplations-in-Action on Wealth," I offer some practical exercises on wealth for those who would like to broaden and deepen their understanding of money and possessions.

12

At times of risk and stress, cultivate stillness

UNCERTAINTY IS WOVEN into everything we do at work: launching a new product, starting a new job, prescribing a drug, even answering the phone. Each day, moment after moment, we deal with work's unknowns by taking risks. Sometimes small risks like accepting a check for a hundred dollars: "Are the funds available or will the check bounce?" Sometimes large risks like performing emergency surgery on an injured child: "Have we diagnosed the injuries correctly? Have we removed all the obstructions or did we miss something? Will the sutures hold?" Uncertainty requires choices, and taking risks is one of work's great demands.

In the face of crisis or risk on the job, we tend to hide out in the extremes of either hesitation or arrogance. Sometimes we underestimate the risks we are taking, failing to appreciate what's at stake. Maybe we are responsible for investing other people's life savings in stocks and bonds. Or maybe we are a CEO and responsible for guiding and growing the assets of a large corporation. The decisions we make in such roles impact thousands of people's lives. It would be the height of arrogance to treat such responsibilities frivolously. Overinvesting others' money in highly speculative funds or, as a CEO, applying "brinkmanship" accounting rules to shore up short-term profits would be blatantly foolhardy. Such overconfidence seriously misjudges the situation, underestimating the unknowns and risks.

On the other hand, we may overestimate the risks we are taking, exaggerating their importance. Maybe the very same financial investor invests his client's money too conservatively, getting a poor return on the investment. There are opportunities to consider—market segments that have strong track records, funds that are diversified sufficiently to prudently manage the risks—but he hesitates: "Maybe the market will go south tomorrow. Let me look at the companies' balance sheets once again. Maybe next week I'll run my risk/reward performance-predictor software on these investment ideas to see whether they are likely to perform or not." Or our CEO may not be willing to compete aggressively when confronted with marketplace pressures. Maybe she hesitates to invest in new product development or new technology to keep pace with change. Instead she hires a consulting firm to study the issue and make recommendations. She schedules a meeting in three weeks to hear new ideas and proposals. When we overestimate our risks, blowing them out of proportion, fearful of possible outcomes, we freeze and become indecisive. Such hesitation or lack of confidence is ponderous and halting, overestimating the unknowns and risks.

In order to avoid these extremes of arrogance and hesitation, we first have to be clear about what we are dealing with. When we take risks, we find ourselves feeling a range of powerful emotions. We can feel intrigued, bedeviled, excited, or afraid. The greater the risk we feel we are taking, the more complex and challenging our feelings. We should not regard these powerful emotions as problems or distractions, however. Rather, they are our natural instincts, our inborn intelligence, which can help us manage uncertainty, *if we know how to listen.* If we try to ignore them, treating them like distractions or unneeded worries, we are probably being overconfident and may be underestimating the risks. If we pay too much attention to our feelings, constantly agonizing over possibilities, chances are we are hesitating, lacking confidence, and possibly overestimating the risks. Properly listening to our emotions at times of crisis or risk in order to learn why they want our attention requires balance and poise.

To gain such composure at stressful moments, we can apply the mindfulness effort of letting go—abruptly shifting our attention from our thoughts to the immediacy of our physical environment. By suddenly being mindful in this way, we discover a visceral stillness, an "emotional space" of *not knowing,* like opening a door to an unfamiliar room or leaping from a diving board. When we are mindful in the immediate moment, the chaotic flood of emotions no longer vies for our attention like a crowd of loud, unruly voices. Instead, they focus and settle into a physical feeling, unclear and murky, but no less powerful—a tickle in the stomach, a vague softness around the heart, or an openness in the throat. Our senses, on the other hand, become extraordinarily vivid. The sound of the phone ringing is precise and distinct. The humidity or coolness of the air is no longer the background but is fully experienced. Our worn briefcase in all its familiarity is rich in detail. We discover that our emotions are actually bodily instincts—visceral, available, and informative. And our alertness gives us the precision and confidence needed to act.

By shifting our attention to our physical setting during times of crisis or risk, we acknowledge that our familiar feelings of control are gone and, ironically, we are at the same time alert and instinctively open to our circumstances, surprisingly calm and even. Such a space can be uncomfortable, since there are no familiar emotional signposts or reliable answers, and our impulse to seek assurances and closure can become quite strong. Our mindfulness practice, however, trains us to pause and rest in the "stillness of the unfamiliar." For a moment we have nothing to hold on to—we are just instinctively alert, resourceful, and open to the situation.

By stepping past our desire to resolve our emotions and making friends with this stillness, we finally discover the basis for making tough and risky decisions. From this open space, we can acknowledge our anxieties and powerful emotions in a balanced way, letting them play their role of alerting us to possibilities. The tickle in the stomach may remind us to call our most important client before making a critical investment. Seemingly out of nowhere we understand how best to finance a competitive bid. We experience a wave of relief, a physical calm, and we make the call and close the deal. A lingering doubt makes us check one last time before we close the accident victim's leg wound, and sure enough, we discover a small shard of glass. Over time we discover that our emotions and bodily sensations are actually guiding, not distracting our decisions, prompting us to consider our gut feeling more deliberately and respectfully. We learn to listen through the stillness to our feelings, our work setting, our competitors, our colleagues. By learning to remain still in unfamiliar territory, we discover that we are expressing the very confidence that we have been seeking all along: a confidence guided by instinct and insight that is free from the anxiety of hesitation or the blindness of arrogance.

Developing our ability to listen to our emotions and body during times of stress and risk requires that we train thoroughly in mindfulness disciplines. Besides sitting meditation, the most effective technique I have used for listening deeply to the physical wisdom of the body is a practice called Focusing, developed by Dr. Eugene Gendlin from the University of Chicago. Gene and his colleague, Dr. Flavia Cymbalista, an economist from the Berlin Free University, spent many hours training and coaching me in listening to the language of the body as it seeks to guide and inspire decisions. I highly recommend learning this method of focusing as a powerful tool for making sound financial decisions, unblocking pent-up creativity, resolving conflicts, or just listening deeply to what your body is trying to tell you. (See my Web site www.AwakeAt Work.net for more information on this technique.)

"At times of risk and stress, cultivate stillness" proposes no magic for making difficult decisions and taking risks. We will need to be thorough and realistic. We will need to work through difficulties and make mistakes. At times we will need to have the courage of our convictions and possibly take risks that complicate our lives and those of others. But most of all, we will need to trust our inherent confidence to remain still in unfamiliar territory, listening deeply and precisely.

13

Cultivate "kitchen sink" mentality

ALL OF US have been in unclean kitchens. Maybe at college
we were a bit sloppy or our housemates ignored such things
and our kitchens were grimy and unpleasant places to visit.
Or maybe we stopped at a roadside diner once and noticed the
chef sneezing onto the oily grill where our burger was sizzling.
Lingering in such places can make us feel sickened and unsettled. The sour odors and sticky floors, the overflowing garbage
cans and the unrefrigerated foods offend us, and we feel that
we want to escape from something that is deeply and viscerally
wrong.

In cleaning up such a kitchen, one of the very first things
we would do is check that the kitchen sink was prepared
for the job. We would make sure we had enough dish soap,
sponges, and steel wool pads. We would scrub the sink and its
counter and maybe use some bleach to eliminate any bacteria
and contamination. As we worked, the kitchen sink would
become intimate, dependable, and familiar: the slightly loose
faucet, the shelf holding the soap, the worn drain. Having
a clean kitchen sink would make the clutter and garbage

suddenly seem less complicated. Despite the sour odors and sticky floors, we could start to feel more optimistic.

Kitchen sinks help us treat our world properly. We can pay attention to details and produce a meal. When we are clean and thorough, we can offer a wholesome place for people to converse and eat, and clean up afterward. As we rinse the vegetables, wipe the cutting boards, scrape the plates, and wash each dish and utensil with hot water, we feel fresh and satisfied by the feeling of doing things thoroughly and well. Such a kitchen sink mentality can be a profound way to be in the world.

Cultivating a kitchen sink mentality encourages us to treat our mind like the kitchen sink in our pursuit of livelihood. Rather than attending to problems by using "everything *but* the kitchen sink," we actually *begin* with "kitchen sink mentality": fresh, orderly, and complete. We first develop a precise and thorough approach to the basics. Is our desk arranged neatly? Do we relate to supplies, tools, or files precisely? Do we follow through on what we say? Are we attentive to our clothing and manners, and do we speak clearly and deliberately? Does everything have its place, and are we seen as clean, clear, and precise in a complicated and unruly work world?

By cultivating such precision, we can feel wholesome and free from doubt and complication in relating to our colleagues at work. We begin to take great satisfaction in doing things properly. Since we are willing to be conscientious and tidy, people come to us, not just because we can solve their problems, but because we express a natural sense of wholesomeness. We are not afraid of the workplace's sticky pots and pans or dirty refrigerator. Our colleagues find such confidence trustworthy and inspiring.

Kitchen sink mentality naturally cares for the world and

takes satisfaction in doing things correctly—not in the sense that we want to take responsibility from others and try to solve all the world's problems, but because we feel a desire to clean up our world and not leave a mess for others. Such sentiments are not wishful thinking; they are as instinctive and personal as wanting to keep *ourselves* clean and healthy. My teacher, Chögyam Trungpa Rinpoche, placed a high premium on kitchen sink mentality. It was in attending to life's messy, routine details that he encouraged us to seek "enlightened mind." Life's "vicissitudes," as he would wryly call the difficulties of daily existence, required that we be thorough, wakeful, and fresh, expressing our natural decency and authenticity. At the heart of cultivating a kitchen sink mentality is a profound respect for a world that has become vividly familiar to us: our work and our world are our home and the home for many others. Being precise and thorough and fresh is not a problem. It's the natural thing to do.

14

Be kind to yourself

WE CAN BE pretty hard on ourselves at work. A lot is expected of us, and measuring up to expectations puts pressure on us to perform. We want to be seen as competent and capable—and then we have to live up to our *own* aspirations. Tight timetables, complex challenges, risky decisions, and much more can keep us going at a pace that is just asking too much. "Be kind to yourself" suggests that we lighten up a bit, that we slow down and treat ourselves decently.

The basics of being kind to yourself is simply "having a cup of tea." We can do so quite literally—taking a break and enjoying a cup of tea, savoring the flavors and aroma, perhaps with a cookie or a cracker and cheese. We slow down and give ourselves an open moment where we can appreciate the world around us with no agenda. Whether it's a tea break, a stroll at the local park, or a moment at the water cooler, being kind to ourselves at its most basic level invites us to deliberately step away from the pace of work and enjoy the simple pleasures of being alive.

Being kind to ourselves also encourages us to view work as our spiritual path rather than just a scorecard. We are going to have some great successes at work. Just as important, we are going to make mistakes as well—some minor and workable, some serious and difficult to manage. Granted, keeping track of our mistakes and missteps at work is part of the territory. But keeping score need not be our primary focus. When work becomes our spiritual path, we admit that work is messy, that we will make mistakes, and that our mistakes are vital to how we learn. Being kind to ourselves suggests that we need not beat ourselves up over errors in judgment, political blunders, or oversights in performing our work. We are on a path to learn how to be awake at work, and our mistakes are key lessons in doing just that. Rather than being hard on ourselves because of mistakes, being kind to ourselves invites us to take a fresh view, learn our lesson, and go forward—ventilating our world as we go. When we are hard on ourselves, we are inevitably hard on others. Kindness to ourselves clears the air for everyone around us: colleagues, friends, and family.

Finally, being kind to ourselves invites us to relax. Not just to kick back and light up a cigar or have a cocktail, though this could be fine at the right place and time. *Relax* in the sense that we can drop the burden of maintaining our point of view. At times of pressure, we can find ourselves being defensive or rigid—maybe taking ourselves a bit too seriously. Maybe we have to hold our ground on changing a critical deadline or one of our project team members is throwing a tantrum and blaming us for a deskful of problems. Being kind to ourselves suggests that we can lay down the heavy burden of taking a stand. We can afford to lighten up and listen and adjust—to be with the situation even if it is sticky and unpleasant. Being kind to ourselves invites us to appreciate that whenever work—and life in general—does not go the way we want it to, we can pause, put our heavy bags down, give ourselves a "cup of tea," and remember that we are not just doing a job but are being awake at work.

15

Open

WHEN WE ARE awake at work, we engage our everyday circumstances from a simple yet powerful perspective: we are *open*. Without our rehearsals, we are mindful and available, precise in our conduct, and familiar with our feelings and instincts. Our mind and body and our physical setting synchronize, and our jobs become both art and science, spontaneous and planned, relaxing and demanding. By being open at our job, we also discover that our work setting cannot be taken for granted. Where we find ourselves is not just a passing landscape, removed and somewhat two-dimensional. Our desk and tools, customers and colleagues, lunch counter and elevator, all share and display a lively intelligence that weaves through each moment and in all directions. We discover that not only are *we* open but the situation is profoundly open as well: vivid, inviting, and strangely playful.

Waking up to this mutual openness is something that can and does happen quite naturally, requiring no other technique than simply being human. Just noticing a fall leaf tumble to the pavement or the steam gently rise from a hot cup of coffee can immediately reveal the vastness of this life. Sometimes, particularly when work's tone and pace seem to slow down, we may choose to deliberately remind ourselves to wake up: to be open and acknowledge the openness of our work setting.

At any time during our day we can open ourselves by using the following four simple steps, which I discuss below: 1. Notice, pause, and breathe. 2. Acknowledge mutual openness. 3. Get back to work. 4. Stay open.

Notice, Pause, and Breathe

Being open starts with stopping our minds. We can do so by being mindful of just about anything. Our shoe might be untied; our boss may be walking quickly out the door; a computer screen flickers; a dog barks. And suddenly we notice that our world is simply and energetically *happening*. Noticing the sheer immediacy stops our minds instantly. Such moments are signals for us to relax further, to slow down even further. Once we stop and notice the immediate moment, we naturally pause. It's as if there were a gentle invitation to linger—a restful sense that there is nothing to do, nowhere to go. Normally we rush past this pause. Out of anxiety or habit, out of blindness or just speed, we miss the invitation to pause and quickly become removed from the immediacy, talking to ourselves or becoming absorbed in a task once again. But in this case, we deliberately acknowledge the pause by taking a long, deep, unhurried breath.

Acknowledge Mutual Openness

By taking a breath, we accept the invitation to linger with the restful sense of just being present. Lingering in the moment—

even for just a split second—can be very personal and touching. There is sharpness to our alertness, yet there is a calm personal warmth as well—a calm alertness. From such a perspective, we consciously acknowledge that we are no longer closed off from our world. Our inner rehearsals, the speed of our job, the worries and firefighting, are not closing us off for that moment; we are simply open, and surprisingly our world is open as well. So open that the world is not what we thought it was all along, so open that our experience is beyond watcher and watched, us and it, before and after. For a split second we may glimpse the vastness of being awake. And then we gently acknowledge this openness, as if quietly within ourselves we joined our hands and gently bowed our heads in respect. At such a moment, we may even be so fortunate as to recognize such openness as an old, old friend.

Get Back to Work

Once we acknowledge this mutual openness, we bring our attention back to the tasks at hand; we literally "get back to work." We do this not to dismiss or ignore the openness but to avoid confining it. By lingering too long with acknowledging openness, we might make the mistake of solidifying our experience, making openness an object of curiosity rather than what it actually is: this very moment completely free from any agenda or reference points. By getting back to work, we drop any attachment to our experience of openness and let ourselves freely engage our work circumstances as they unfold. Sometimes we may remain open as we get back to work: our body, mind, and action remain synchronized and we engage our job with a heightened awareness that lacks any self-consciousness or hesitation. At other times we may become distracted by work's speed and excitement. Running the old commentaries, rushing past the present moment, we simply forget to be open. Either way is fine—we simply get back to work.

Stay Open

Staying open is not a matter of achieving anything, of trying to be present for longer and longer periods of time. Rather, staying open is appreciating that openness happens with or without our even noticing it. Over time we come to understand that being open is not an option that we can turn on and off like a light switch but a condition of being alive. We may space out, forget, get absorbed in our anger or anxiety, or simply mindlessly distract ourselves from the immediate moment, but we cannot escape. Our feet still touch the ground and our head still turns right and left; we cannot avoid such things. The present moment stays open with or without our attention. We stay open, then, because there is no other option.

Of course, this may sound a bit too cute—too koanlike: "You stay open even when you are not open. Staying open happens even when you close up." Being skeptical of such things makes a lot of sense: we should never buy such a bill of goods without testing it for ourselves. If we doubt such a thing—that we have no option but to stay open even when we are closed—we can do a simple test: stop our mind, notice the black ink on this white page, take a long, unhurried breath, and simply acknowledge whatever happens next.

PART THREE

WORKING WITH OTHERS

The eleven slogans in this section suggest that we can dismantle any resistance or resentment we may have toward our colleagues at work and take a fresh, skillful, and decent approach to working with others.

- Welcome the tyrant
- First to pacify, last to destroy
- No blame
- Practice "no credentials"
- Cultivate the art of conversation
- Avoid idiot compassion
- Study the six confusions
- Extend the four composures
- Everybody just wants to bounce their ball

- Treat everyone as a guest
- Witness from the heart

When we mix these slogans with our daily jobs, we recognize that resisting work's inevitable human conflicts only confuses matters more, making us ineffective and unhelpful and possibly creating the very conflicts we seek to avoid. By dropping fixed views of ourselves—our status, credentials, and authority—we permit ourselves to open to conflicts, to be inquisitive rather than resistant, flexible rather than rigid, insightful rather than "correct." The eleven slogans of the "Working with Others" section point out that the colleagues we meet at work—coworkers, customers, clients, vendors, managers, and subordinates—are all our spiritual teachers, pointing the way to being awake at work. As such, they are worthy of our deepest gratitude and respect.

16

Welcome the tyrant

PEOPLE AT WORK can be unusually irritating. For many reasons, we can find ourselves offended or angry with colleagues: a coworker who publicly accepts praise for a job well done by others; a condescending customer who never seems satisfied; a supplier who is full of polite excuses for never getting a delivery right; or worst of all, an overbearing and unapologetic boss. We can become peculiarly insulted by such behavior, losing our emotional balance, often in complete disproportion to the actual importance of the slight. At times our colleagues can seem like tyrants, having a unique power to unsettle us and keep us up at night.

Typically, when we feel oppressed by tyrants, we struggle and we try to reassure ourselves that we are not to blame, that we do not deserve such insults and injustices. We may complain to our spouses or partners about how we are treated. The more we struggle, the more the insult seems to expand; the more we ponder the tyrant, the more disturbing he becomes. We may find ourselves plotting retaliation, waiting in ambush to offer cutting insights into our tyrant's treacherous ways. In the meantime, we go about our business uneasy and on guard, keeping ourselves protected and unavailable. Tyrants have a way of making us feel uncomfortable in our very own skins.

When we examine them closely, we discover that tyrants are simply mirrors of our own insecurities and fears. Our own doubts and worries distort challenging relationships into circumstances that can terrorize us. In reality, tyrants are simply ordinary, messy work circumstances blown out of proportion by our lack of confidence. Because we are worried about the *possibility* of losing our job, an unruly boss gains unusual power over us—becoming a tyrant. Because we are anxious about the *possibility* of being perceived as ineffective, our showboating colleague gains unusual power over us—becoming a tyrant. Because we are troubled about the *possibility* that our job could get out of control, our condescending customer seems to have our future in her hands—becoming a tyrant. Tyrants are stark invitations to look in the mirror and examine our futile search for security in an uncertain workplace.

Recognizing that we are, in fact, authoring our tyrants— that our hopes and fears are what fuel their power over us—is central to regaining our balance. In the Buddhist tradition, coming upon such irritating and oppressive people is highly valued. Any life circumstance that can expose our insecurities is considered a gift to be welcomed and explored.

One might well ask: "Why would I want to befriend such rude people? Why would I welcome such a mess into my life?" But welcoming the tyrant need not be so distasteful. Such a task, at its core, can be quite simple and direct. To welcome the tyrant, we must be willing to let go of our inner defensiveness—even for a brief moment—and experience our tyrants without bias or preconception. Typically, tyrants make us tighten our grip on our viewpoints and justifications. Tyrants control us by making us hold on and defend ourselves. Here we do the opposite; we let go instead of holding on. By suddenly shifting our mind-set, we disarm our tyrants. Our inner insecurities no longer empower our tormentors, giving us the chance to see our circumstances clearly.

A sales executive who was attending an Awake at Work seminar once said to me: "Welcoming the tyrant sounds great. But I can't be honest with my boss. He is so aggressive, yelling and interrogating at staff meetings, no one dares confront him. I'm sure he would fire me on the spot if I spoke my mind openly and honestly."

Such is our fear of tyrants. If we were actually to confront them, we would be inviting their sloppy wrath, the last thing we want! But such confrontation is not really necessary. Welcoming the tyrant does not require that we suddenly release all our pent-up frustrations toward our boss in the middle of a staff meeting. It begins as a simple inner gesture. My suggestion was only this: "At the next meeting, just for a moment, let go of all your fixed ideas about your boss and just be there in the room. Be curious and notice what's going on. Welcome the situation."

A few weeks passed, and this executive spoke to me again after class: "Well, I took your advice," she said. "For just a brief moment, I dropped my resentment toward my boss at the staff meeting and just observed. Sure enough, for that moment I wasn't preoccupied with his being such an idiot, and I could see what was really going on."

"What did you see?" I asked.

"Well, first off, he was in a hurry—he seemed to need to be somewhere else. He wasn't listening and he seemed very distracted. He seemed so unhappy being in the meeting, or at least that's how it looked."

"What about the other people in the room—your sales managers? What did you notice there?"

"I hadn't really noticed this before, but they were just going through a routine. Everything seemed so staged and insincere. Oh, and I also noticed that they were holding back a lot of good news. One of my guys deliberately avoided telling all of us about a major sale he had just closed. It dawned on me that even telling good news had become too much of a risk. And my best sales manager looked bored out of her mind. For a moment I thought that maybe she was thinking of getting a job somewhere else."

"So what did you learn?" I asked.

"Well, my boss still makes me uptight, that's for sure. But I can drop it and, at least for a moment, see the situation without my anxiety. I had been missing a lot: my managers are holding back, the good news is not being told, and my best sales manager is bored by the whole mess."

This sales executive had learned that welcoming the tyrant was an exercise in simply being curious about what oppressed her. Much to her surprise, her tyrant had become disarmed—just for a moment. The blinding effects of her own anxieties had diminished and she could get a clearer picture of what was really going on—with herself, her boss, and her sales team.

By welcoming the tyrant in this way over and over again, we gradually become relaxed with dropping our insecurities about those who irritate us. We discover that much of what bothers us is of our own making. The colleague who doesn't say "good morning" is not insulting us. We look closer and find that his personal life has unraveled and he is soon to be divorced. He comes in sad and withdrawn—not rude and insulting. The new employee who interrupts at meetings is not disrespectful. We look closer and find that she is just nervous and awkwardly trying to fit in. We begin to see that many of the workplace's perceived slights are not slights at all.

Welcoming the tyrant sharpens our intelligence and confidence, making us more effective and versatile. Over time our anxiety toward tyrants dissolves, transforming into an astute curiosity. Why is our colleague embarrassing herself publicly by taking credit where none is due? What in our boss's life makes him so angry and aloof and arrogant toward his subordinates? By welcoming the tyrant, we learn to examine oppressive circumstances very closely, not push them away—to welcome the tyrant, not destroy him. By doing so, we find a courage that frees us to be remarkably skillful in managing irritating work circumstances.

17

First to pacify, last to destroy

MANAGING WORKPLACE conflicts and difficult business problems can be challenging. We may need to give tough feedback to a colleague or motivate a subordinate who has become disillusioned and upset. Or maybe our business is not doing well, and we need to cut costs and lay off employees. Maybe we have missed a deadline that has disturbed our boss and confused our customer and we need to clear the air quickly and get back on track. Such difficulties are unavoidable at work.

Many of us try to avoid these problems by treading lightly and being overly friendly or optimistic. Bad news or differences of opinion can make us rigid and defensive, refusing to accept responsibility, unable to listen, learn, or adjust. Conflict can make us arrogant and dismissive, or it can make us feel like a failure or that we are disliked. Relating to conflict and difficulties, however, need not be so distressing. Managing conflicts skillfully—being responsible, making sound decisions, being inventive, helping others—can be a powerful opportunity for growing both professionally and spiritually. A traditional Buddhist way to work effectively with conflict is to apply what is called the Mahakala principle.

In Tibetan Buddhism, the Mahakala is a familiar yet disturbing image, a fierce being with four arms, adorned with bones and weapons. Striking a threatening and regal pose, the Mahakala is the Tibetan version of a guardian angel. Meditators rely on his powers to help them work with conflicts and difficulties of all kinds in their daily lives. Yet the Mahakala is no creature that is believed to be floating around in some heaven or hell or slinking about in our backyard. He is much closer to us than that. The Mahakala is so real and powerful because he represents our innate ability to promote what is right and sane and to eliminate what is wrong and harmful. Doing what is right and refraining from what is wrong is quite commonplace: we do it every day. We don't throw trash into our neighbor's yard; we don't steal from the local grocer. We lend a hand when necessary and we teach our children to be respectful. Why, then, is such natural behavior represented by such a disquieting image?

The Mahakala's fierce pose is a warning: being impulsive or arrogant about knowing what is right and what is wrong, especially during conflict, can be disastrous! We may only be seeking the best for everyone, but insisting on what is "correct" for others without having fully appreciated the entire situation can be the height of arrogance and can result in lost opportunities, broken friendships, or even wars. The Mahakala takes a fierce pose to alert us to such risks: Manage conflicts and difficulties precisely. Doing what is right and decent leaves no room for sloppiness or frivolity.

If we were to examine the four-armed Mahakala more closely, we would see that he carries four weapons: a skull cup

ༀ། དགར་ནག་མེ་ལྡན་ཁྱབ་འབེ་རབ་གས། པདམ་ཉི་ཟླ་རོ་ལེ་སྟེ་དབ། །

ཁྲག་ག་ཚིག་གསུག་བནེ་སྟེ་དམ་ཕྱི་ལམ་བཞུག་ས། ཁྲ་མ་པོ་ཆེ་ན་པོ་ཕྱུག་གར་ཚ་ལག།

Four-Armed Mahakala.

filled with a magical medicine, a hooked knife, a sword, and a three-pointed spear, or trident. These four weapons represent four inner resources we have for skillfully working with conflict, traditionally called the four actions: pacifying, enriching, magnetizing, and destroying.

Pacifying

Pacifying, represented by the skull cup (filled with a calming medicine), is our ability to first work with conflicts gently and peacefully. Often we see business difficulties as confrontations, filled with unruly energy and unknowns. We find ourselves tensing up, physically and psychologically, wanting to eliminate the conflict. We may want to escape the discomfort with excuses or white lies, or resist criticism and defend our views, feeling we have a point to prove.

Pacifying is our ability to drop this entire struggle altogether and choose *first* to be curious about others. When we pacify conflict, we acknowledge that our defensiveness is unnecessary, a psychological weight that is getting in the way of working with the problem. Without it we can focus our attention on the other person and the actual conflict. What is actually at stake here? What does the other person *really* want to say? What would he or she like to see happen? Why is the person so upset, and what would eliminate this distress? Listening, asking questions, appreciating the other's point of view, expressing gratitude, seeking to clarify—all are pacifying activities. Pacifying encourages us to drop our "flight or fight" mentality and apply a gentle, pliant curiosity to conflicts and difficulties. Pacifying sets the foundation for applying the other three actions.

Enriching

Enriching, represented by the hooked knife (which transforms raw material into nourishment), is our ability to support and encourage others—even our adversaries—during conflicts. Typically in conflicts, we prefer to protect *our* territory, preserving *our* resources, voicing *our* opinions, supporting *our* allies, achieving *our* objectives. When we enrich the situation, we recognize that we need not limit ourselves to such a narrow prospect; we can explore a much wider set of possibilities for helping the situation, well beyond simply strengthening and expanding our point of view. Providing perspective, seeking options, promoting win/win solutions, offering assistance, revealing commonalities between positions, making concessions, telling stories that clarify a point, building alliances— all are enriching activities. Once we pacify with gentleness and curiosity, we can be generous and promote sane resolution by inspiring others to feel empowered and supported.

During one assignment in my publishing career, I was asked to take the lead in reorganizing a three-hundred-person global sales force. Many people would be getting new assignments and new managers, and some would be asked to move to new cities and new countries. Some would even lose their jobs altogether. As with all restructuring, people worried about their future, and we worked hard to communicate the new organization quickly so that the sales reps and managers could remain focused on the business and not on anxieties. One sales manager in Europe, Marla, was resisting her new assignment, however—even though her role, location, and responsibilities were essentially unchanged. Over a pleasant dinner in her home city, I listened to her concerns.

Marla did not want to jeopardize her years of hard work

by being reorganized into another role. She had built a loyal customer base in eastern Europe and did not want to confuse her customers with new faces, a bunch of new products, and "flashy" marketing schemes. She was adamant about three issues: she wanted her title to remain the same; she wanted to submit her sales and expense reports to her present finance manager; and she wanted to continue to sell the same product lines to the same customers. From my perspective, these requests were all quite doable—at least for the short term. Permitting her to have her way on these issues wasn't the neat and clean solution that management would have preferred, but her concerns meant a lot to her. To her surprise, I made the following deal with her:

"We really both want the same thing, Marla: we want you to be happy in your job, we want your customers well served, and we want the company's products marketed and sold properly. Let's agree that for the time being you will keep your title and product line as is and keep reporting your finances into the Munich office. But you promise me that we'll meet again in three months and discuss how things are going and you'll keep an open mind. Let's see how things unfold."

Marla had expected me to strong-arm her into the "corporate view" and instead found that her point of view was being accepted. She felt enriched. When, as we had agreed, we met three months later with the reorganization completed, Marla no longer felt so resistant. In fact, she had already implemented many of the new marketing plans and was excited about several of the new product lines. Taking on a new title and finance manager at this point was no longer a problem. In the case of Marla, *enriching* required that the company drop its fixed views and timetables to value her viewpoint and support and encourage her to move forward. By concentrating on shared goals, the atmosphere was enriched enough to build trust and momentum rather than rigidity.

Magnetizing

Magnetizing, represented by the sword (which when wielded focuses attention), is our ability to attract resources during conflicts. Since we dare to give up territory, we can also invite others to do the same. Conflict resolution requires compromise, in which all parties are expected to make concessions, seek alternatives, or trade resources. Magnetizing suggests that because we pacify and enrich, we can draw concessions from others. By modeling our own resourcefulness first, we can then invite others to offer suggestions and share responsibility. Magnetizing seeks contributions and resources from others in order to overcome conflict and difficulty.

During the nineties, profit margins and sales in the video rental business were shrinking, and no amount of marketing seemed to stem the tide. Free rentals, club discounts, extended rental periods, and even free popcorn could not get customers to rent more videos. The customers seemed to have disappeared. Movie studios were predicting the end of video rentals and searching for new partners to distribute their movies. Pay-per-view, satellite TV, video on demand, and cable TV were all being touted as the wave of the future.

Business prospects for home video rentals looked dim until a leading media executive made a keen observation and a truly magnetizing gesture. The executive discovered that video-rental customers hadn't deserted the video stores at all. In fact, the stores were packed with customers, but they were leaving without renting films because the films they wanted to watch were unavailable. Customers typically rented films one to twenty-one days after their initial release in video cassette format, the executive observed, and if the cassettes were not available during that time, customers were unlikely ever to rent that particular movie in the future. The challenge was to provide customers access to newly released films during that twenty-one-day period. Unfortunately only limited numbers of cassettes were available to rent; hence customers were leaving the store empty-handed.

In order to solve the problem, the executive made a bold and magnetizing proposal to all major movie studios: upon initial release of your films on video, give the rental stores unlimited cassettes *for free*.

At first such a proposal seemed preposterous. Studios made money by *selling* videos, not giving them away. In this case, however, the executive was proposing that by supplying unlimited numbers of videos during the first twenty-one days of the new release, no customer would leave the store empty-handed, and sales and profits would soar. In order for this to happen, the studios would have to stop *selling* videos and get into the rental business with the stores. Studios would have to do business very differently, offering their unlimited resources and taking a share of the rental income in return. It did not take long for the studios to do the math; we see the results in our local video stores. New-release movies are available to all customers, and it is rare to see a customer leave a movie-rental store empty-handed. And today, the video-rental business continues to thrive.

By inviting the studios to provide unlimited numbers of cassettes for free, the executive was magnetizing much-needed resources. Rather than becoming hypnotized by the dire circumstances, endlessly cutting costs and defending against industry criticism, the executive first pacified by observing closely what the customer wanted and then magnetized by making an imaginative demand. All concerned came out the better for it: the studios realized improved video income, the stores returned to profitability, and the customers got the films they wanted when they wanted them.

Destroying

The final action of the Mahakala is destroying, represented by the trident, whose three spear prongs destroy anger, possessiveness, and stupidity with one stroke. Destroying is our ability to say NO during conflicts. Because we first pacify the confusion by being open, then enrich everyone's opportunity, and finally magnetize resources and concessions, we have laid the foundation for being tough. We can walk away from a business deal, openly disagree with another's opinion, terminate a project, confront a fraud, or close an entire company because we have had the discipline and heart to first pacify, enrich, and magnetize before destroying.

When we feel defensive or mistreated during times of conflict, we tend to misuse our ability to destroy. Angry words, dismissive attitudes, abrupt and harsh decisions, all arise out of a desire to destroy the conflict or difficulty. Going to "no" as our first resort often only creates further problems. "First to pacify, last to destroy" suggests that we listen first, support others, and seek compromise before we say "You are fired" or "The contract is canceled."

Unfortunately, destroying *first* has become an accepted and at times admired habit among leaders. Take the infamous "Chainsaw" Al Dunlap, the widely celebrated CEO who posed as Rambo on the cover of *USA Today* and titled his 1996 best-seller *Mean Business*. Renowned for his arrogance

and short attention span, "Chainsaw" Al was routinely celebrated on Wall Street in the nineties because of his ability to
ruthlessly "save" businesses such as the Sunbeam Corporation
and Scott Paper. As a CEO, he had shown no loyalty to work-
ers or suppliers, no responsibility to the community, and no
generosity to those less favored. He championed efficiency and
brutality, following no principle other than short-term profits
and cash for himself. There was no room for pacifying, enriching, or magnetizing for "Chainsaw" Al—just destroying.

But chainsawing through difficulties and conflicts creates
only confusion and suffering, which is exactly what the Mahakala warns us against doing. If we are not threatened by conflict, we can take a fresh look at confrontations and be
generous of spirit and intention. We can afford to listen to
others; we can afford to be imaginative. By heeding the Mahakala's suggestion to first pacify, we discover that we are resourceful enough to be daring and available, free from fear and
arrogance. Such confidence knows instinctively what needs
help, what needs to be confronted, and what can be disregarded. "First to pacify, last to destroy" reminds us to sharpen
up during times of conflict—to pay attention. With such alertness we can preserve the sanity of our world even during
extreme discord.

18

No blame

BECAUSE WORK is a mess, it is inevitable that we make mistakes. Some are small, like dialing the wrong number, and some are monumental, like permitting the *Challenger* space shuttle to launch. When we do our jobs well, we try to limit our mistakes. We work hard to accomplish our goals, and we never intentionally mess up. We dislike making mistakes because they create confusion and doubt and can leave us and our colleagues feeling inadequate or embarrassed.

Mistakes require that we retrace our steps, repair damage, and reassess our views. In many instances, mistakes can be our best teachers, demanding that we learn vital lessons about ourselves and how we do our jobs. They require that we stop and consider our circumstances carefully, right here, right now.

At work, unfortunately, mistakes are too often treated more like enemies than teachers. Since they invade our routines, slow us down, cost money, and wreak havoc on plans, the conventional attitude is that mistakes are unacceptable and must be "defeated." We can find ourselves hunting down and punishing mistakes or avoiding them "at all costs." We learn quickly that if mistakes are the enemy, then mistakes are best made by someone else.

When we treat mistakes as enemies rather than teachers, we inevitably end up behaving like cowards. Rather than accepting responsibility, we distance ourselves from problems and difficulties. Rather than facing facts with accountability and precision, we blame or make excuses.

I recall a publishing colleague, Greg, who was uniquely skilled in the art of avoiding responsibility and placing blame. He was renowned as the "Teflon sales manager" because he could cook up endless justifications while ensuring that no mistakes stuck to his record. Greg running a financial meeting was a marvel to behold. If an accountant pointed out that Greg's department was over budget, Greg would calmly recall that he had forecast such an overage six months ago and was surprised that the adjustment had not been made. Or if his travel and entertainment expenses were high, he would patiently remind people that each dollar was targeted to close a critical deal. If someone questioned his low sales forecast, Greg would talk about the realities of "sales cycles." If someone pointed out his escalating marketing costs, Greg would show growing market share. Greg was smooth, confident, and reassuring, and management loved the showmanship. Inevitably, of course, Greg would get cornered, and just as inevitably he would pass the blame on to sales representatives and managers who weren't "pulling their weight." Greg's showmanship was so perfected that when he spoke about the need to fire those who had made the mistakes, he would portray himself as anguished and genuinely troubled. Greg was the supreme Teflon man, and he was also considered by many to be the company's number one coward.

When organizations treat mistakes as the enemy, the results can be disastrous. In the nineties, dozens of companies chose the Teflon route rather than precise accountability: Arthur Andersen, Merrill Lynch, Putnam Investments, Enron, WorldCom, and Global Crossing, among others. Rather than acknowledge business failures and learn from mistakes, hundreds of corporate executives at these firms chose to "restate" profits, book questionable sales, or even manipulate stock prices in order to maintain the facade. Of course, when the criminal charges and lawsuits were filed, no one took responsibility. Others were always to blame. When mistakes are the enemy, the game of hide-and-blame becomes a high art.

"No blame" encourages us to respect errors at work—our own and others'. Of course, we need not announce our failures from atop the tallest building; in fact, being honest about mistakes at work requires tact, humility, and skill. When we permit mistakes to teach us, we discuss problems discreetly and listen to others' points of view. We treat facts as friendly and we learn ways to improve our jobs. We may have to come to some tough conclusions about ourselves and others along the way. When we are honest about mistakes, we slow down and take full stock of our circumstances. This requires us to open ourselves fully to the discomfort and detail, rather than rush past our circumstances, papering over the failures, to regain a false sense of mastery.

"No blame" counteracts the cowardice of avoiding our responsibilities at work. We can bravely learn from our failures without blaming others. Such courage is both demanding and refreshing. Since we are willing to be truthful, precise, and accountable, we are not confused by self-deception. Since we are willing to be honest, there is no struggle.

19

Practice "no credentials"

WORKPLACE CREDENTIALS—our titles, college degrees, qualifications, symbols of status and authority—can sometimes help get the job done and sometimes just get in the way. We trust our physician because she had to graduate from an accredited medical school to earn the MD at the end of her name. Yet we may also be suspicious of doctors, who often seem aloof and unavailable or quick to propose solutions without actually listening. We know that the four-star general has profound responsibility in putting lives at risk. Yet to some of us, military titles and symbols invite doubt and suspicion, possibly even outrage. Our company's CEO seems to be a pleasant fellow, yet even the sound of the title invokes images of arrogance and greed. Credentials of all kinds can build trust or invite suspicion, foster accountability or irresponsibility, communicate expertise or mask weaknesses.

We can never entirely dismiss the value of credentials, of course, but we can learn to keep them in proper perspective by practicing "no credentials." Such a practice begins with noticing how we speak to others about what we do at work and feeling the subtle emotions that run behind our words. For example, at a dinner party or at the local bar, when someone inevitably asks: "So, what do you do?" we may notice that we often answer the question with a noun rather than a verb. Instead of "I teach," we respond, "I am a teacher." Instead of "I build buildings and bridges," we answer, "I am an engineer." Or we may hand the person our business card: "Detective—Homicide Division, Metropolitan Police Force." This apparently insignificant shift of phrasing reminds us that we want to *be someone* at work. We want our jobs and livelihood to shape an identity for us—to provide us a story line of who we are.

We share a beer with a newfound friend and she asks, "So, what do you do?" Perhaps we feel a bit exposed by the question, as if someone had walked into our home unannounced and suddenly sat down at our dinner table. We want to put our best foot forward. When we answer, "I am a divorce lawyer," we don't know what experience our new friend has had with divorces or lawyers in the past, so we feel a bit hesitant, unsure if we are making the right impression. Maybe we are particularly proud of what we do for a living, maybe a bit embarrassed. We may respond with poise and restraint, "I am the president of Costa Rica," or lower our heads and mumble, "I am the dishwasher and chef at the Moldy Bottom Lounge and Restaurant," or even, "I am a stay-at-home mom." For many of us, answering the question "So, what do you do?" is like walking onto life's stage for a moment to make a fundamental statement about who we are.

How we portray ourselves to others—the workplace "story line" that we live in words, feelings, and deeds—is of primary importance in practicing "no credentials." By carefully examining our story lines, we actually feel the emotions we invest in needing to be someone at work: the vague relief when we are introduced as "Vice President So and So," the tightness in our chest or tone of voice when we respond to a customer who dismisses us rudely, or the sense of loneliness when we hear others discuss their college education—an education we never had. When we practice "no credentials," we sharply examine such feelings in order to uncover any smugness, impoverishment, defensiveness, or blindness we may be harboring as part of how we conduct ourselves at work. In doing so, we confront one of the great obstacles to being authentic and effective at work: mistakenly thinking we are our job.

Coming to the conclusion that we are what is written on our business card or printed on our paycheck is an understandable occupational hazard, however. We invest so much in our jobs—forty, fifty, or more hours a week, personal commitment, creative effort. In fact, we invest our lives. Yet, despite our generous investment, our jobs cannot offer us a true identity. Harbormaster, cabdriver, owner, nurse—these titles cannot offer us a fixed view of ourselves or our world. Like everything else at work, credentials are fluid and constantly changing. Try as we might, we cannot create a seamless, reliable version of ourselves out of our career or job. And when we expect otherwise—when we expect work to deliver something it can never deliver—we become frustrated and uptight: exaggerating achievements, glossing over failures, sugarcoating mistakes; feeling arrogant, slighted, embarrassed, or smug.

By practicing "no credentials," we are willing to examine these feelings candidly, gradually unraveling the blinding effects of clinging to our credentials. We learn to let go of job titles and pretense and shift our attention to being authentic, to being who we are, where we are, at work.

In dropping our preoccupation with credentials, we begin

to rely more on our natural instincts and curiosity. We naturally become more curious about others than about ourselves.

When we practice "no credentials" as a fast-food server, for example, we know that we are not our uniform; we are not the story line. We may feel detached or uneasy about having a minimum-wage job, and the uniform we are wearing may be tight fitting and awkward. But, for a moment, we can let go of the fast-food-server story line and notice our world. We see people of all kinds—young and old; rich and poor; black, brown, yellow, and white—who are hungry. We begin to understand and appreciate our world from this perspective. Some people are rushed and rude, others courteous, still others indecisive or distracted. Some seem to have little money to afford their meal. All wait in line—hungry—wanting to order something to eat. As a fast-food server, we can uniquely and intimately appreciate this world. We become a kind of expert on the behavior of hungry people. By practicing "no credentials" in this way, we discover the poetry of our job and begin to become deeply curious about our world rather than preoccupied with ourselves. We discover that our credentials actually provide us with a wider view of the world rather than just a story line.

Of course, practicing "no credentials" is not limited to those of us who work in fast-food restaurants.

Dr. John Coleman was the former president of the Federal Reserve Bank of Philadelphia, one of twelve reserve banks that make up the central bank of the United States. As president of the bank, Dr. Coleman was a member of a small team of strategists responsible for setting financial policy that had profound influence on lives throughout the United States and the world. Their decisions affected everything from the cost of a first-grade education to the tonnage of free wheat shipped to underdeveloped nations to the cost of a square foot of new highway. But Dr. Coleman did not permit his impeccable qualifications and power to blind him. His upbringing as a Quaker taught him that his status and title were as much an obstacle to the truth as a vehicle for understanding it. Relying solely on the rarified dominion of the Federal Reserve Bank presidency, with its staff of economists modeling statistical views of the world, was not sufficient for him. In order to get a true picture of the world that he was so profoundly influencing, to be authentic as a president, he needed to fully appreciate other people's lives—their struggles and joys, their hopes and fears. So Dr. Coleman took occasional time out "to walk in other people's shoes," as he put it, traveling the country to dig ditches, collect garbage, work in mines, labor in emergency rooms, and at one point live destitute on the streets of New York City. As the president of the Federal Reserve Bank of Philadelphia, Dr. Coleman practiced "no credentials." He let go of his status, power, title, and qualifications, and he engaged the world *on its terms*—from a fresh perspective of interested curiosity.

We may not have the time to literally go on the road and walk in other people's shoes—though many people do just that as part of their spiritual practice. But we can make a practice out of genuinely considering the other person's point of view. The bridge construction worker at the roadside as we speed past at sixty miles per hour: what is it like for him to be out there twisting a steel girder into place in ten-degree weather? The politician on CNN trying to explain why she should be reelected—how does it feel to have such ambition and be so relentlessly "onstage" all the time? The customer on the telephone line confused and disheartened about receiving the wrong product for the third time—what kind of frustration must he be experiencing? The systems analyst nervously presenting the cost-benefit study: how genuine and well-meaning her uneasiness is. By being humble enough to drop our story line and carefully consider others, we develop a powerful flexibility of mind and heart that not only instructs us in how the world works but also inspires trust and mutual respect.

By practicing "no credentials," we discover how to be truly responsible. Appreciating how others feel as secretaries, chemists, priests, and cops makes us even more aware of how people rely on us, whether to serve fast food properly or to run a bank that helps eliminate poverty. By practicing "no credentials," we discover that to be who we are, where we are, at work is simply to appreciate others and do the best job we can.

20

Cultivate the art of conversation

A COMMON WORKPLACE image nowadays is a man or woman staring slack-jawed at a computer, tapping and twitching at the keyboard. Many of us could see ourselves in that picture. Whether we are buried in a newspaper or a computer screen, glancing at a cell phone or watching television, the scene is pretty much the same: a lone person staring at a device and poking at it on occasion. We have quietly grown accustomed to engaging our world as bits of information. We scan printed words and pictures, watch TV newspeople describe life, push buttons to go to digitalized landscapes. Such an approach to engaging work—indeed our lives—has become common, at times preferred. But the image of the lone person mesmerized by the computer illustrates a central risk to the modern workplace and should come with a dire warning: Information is addictive and may make you unavailable to reality.

Of course, operating computers and managing information are critical to contributing at work. We all want to be facile with such things. Information can bring efficiency and scope to our lives, making everything from governments to kindergartens run more effectively. Vast access to information gives us a formidable command of our world, empowering us to accomplish more in one day than our ancestors could in an entire lifetime. But when we substitute a digital game for life's rawness, data for genuine communication, and digital dialogue for heartfelt human contact, we can cut ourselves off from our world. We anesthetize ourselves, distort our sense of priorities, and become unavailable to others. One way to avoid this numbing quality of today's technology is to "cultivate the art of conversation."

A good conversation, whether at work or elsewhere, is one of life's great gifts. Whether we are listening to an amusing story unfold or recounting a tender and insightful moment, talking with friends and colleagues can be a great delight. Even in this modern information society, a good conversation continues to be one of the most effective and enjoyable ways to learn. Having a cup of tea with a neurosurgeon will likely yield more insights into spinal cord research than days spent exploring the Web. Talking with a politician can give us a truer measure of where she stands than hours of reading campaign literature. And in the course of such conversations, we run the delightful chance of making a friend.

At work, however, we typically converse in order to get somewhere—to achieve things. So much of our conversation is taken up with deliverables, deadlines, and crises that much of the art of conversation is overlooked. We may be getting somewhere in our conversations, but by not also *being* somewhere, we can miss the graceful role conversations play in promoting a decent, respectful, and creative workplace. Cultivating the art of conversation encourages us to consider our exchanges at work not just as opportunities to be effective and get our job done but also as valuable moments to be considerate, alert, and authentic.

In order to cultivate this art, we can keep in mind the following courtesies of workplace conversations.

Notice the Setting

Taking note of our physical surroundings creates space for our conversation: we slow down and appreciate the moment. By noticing where we are, we may choose to have a conversation elsewhere out of earshot of others, straighten up our desk to create a more appealing atmosphere, or simply meet the moment fully alert.

Appreciate Silence

Conversations are inevitably punctuated with moments of silence. Such pauses can be slightly unnerving, but we can refrain from filling them up. We can pause and respect the moment, letting the situation unfold at its own pace.

Stop Talking and Listen Deeply

The greatest mistake we can make in a conversation is not to listen. Rambling on, getting through the conversation, repeating our point of view, spacing out, assuming we know what the other person is about to say—in effect trying to *get somewhere fast*—is simply insulting. Much that is communicated at work is not spoken. Our colleagues' tone of voice, body posture, choice of phrases—even the placement of a briefcase or a pen—can offer insights into what is truly being said and what our colleagues truly need. By listening deeply, we are fully available and attentive and invite others to be equally open.

Ask Helpful Questions

Conversations are as much about helping others make their points as they are about making our own. Expressing our genuine curiosity with questions and statements that clarify, summarize, draw parallels, build consensus—generally helping the dialogue take shape and meaning—shows respect for all involved.

Speak Clearly, Refraining from Harsh Phrases and Jargon

Using profanities and demeaning language at work destroys trust and respect among colleagues. Ironically, using jargon can have the same effect. Saying to a colleague, "Your PC's installation to the RP real-time constellation network will begin Friday," rather than, "We'll be networking your computer this weekend," creates doubt in our abilities and disregard for our opinions. Speaking clearly and straightforwardly—using an economy of speech when practical moments demand clarity—invites the same in return and is the mark of a clear and present mind.

Have a Sense of Humor

Enjoying ourselves in conversation is just plain human. Not taking ourselves too seriously, clearing the air with helpful anecdotes, retelling an instructive story, are all part of the poetry and art of good conversation. We need not be stand-up comedians, but keeping our dialogue fresh and playful, open to unseen twists and offhand comments, is a way to be vividly present in the midst of work's constant pace to get things done.

Appreciate Coincidence

Conversations inevitably lead to unseen possibilities. How many times in a conversation have we said things like "I didn't know you worked with her at XYZ Company!" or "I've contracted for the same services—there is no reason why we can't coordinate our market research and save some bucks," or "I'll be in Boston next week too—why don't we go on the sales call together?" Conversations yield potentially fruitful coincidences—the natural outcome of the art.

While these suggested courtesies may be helpful, cultivating the art of conversation is far more than a set of rules: it is a profound human capacity for bringing the best out of others and for expressing our own authenticity. Our conversations can preserve the humanity of work in the midst of today's numbing blizzard of technology, speed, and ambition. We can actually take a moment—in fact hundreds of moments a day—to enliven our mutual humanity by noticing and listening to one another. By deliberately being alert and available in our conversations, we show respect toward our colleagues, promoting an atmosphere that cultivates *li* and inspires trust. Cultivating the art of conversation then becomes an exercise in the joy of balancing effort—being thoroughly present and getting the job done.

21

Avoid idiot compassion

WHEN WE SEE our fellow colleagues having difficulties at work, we naturally want to lend a hand. Sometimes work's demands are weighing heavily on a colleague, or maybe a new challenge has someone stumped and we give a bit of advice or direction in order to help out. Sometimes we put in extra effort, staying late at work to help meet a deadline or coming in early to set up for a meeting. Helping could be as simple as just listening as someone thinks out loud about whether to accept a new job or move to Arizona. Helping others is a natural and necessary part of work.

Helping others at work, however, is not always as simple as it may seem. Sometimes we can't help. If we have a lot to do and don't have the time, we have to leave problems for others to solve. Or maybe we have to resist helping out because doing someone else's job only creates confusion about who's responsible for what. Many problems are simply beyond our abilities, and offering advice or assistance might make matters worse. So helping at work often requires us *not to help*—to refrain from offering advice, to leave questions unanswered, to let

colleagues struggle with problems. Being helpful at work actually requires enormous skill and timing—knowing when to
listen, when to walk away, when to take command, when to
learn rather than teach.

If we are not skillful at helping others at work, we can find
ourselves working really hard at being helpful when if fact we
are creating a greater mess. My teacher Chögyam Trungpa
Rinpoche called this *idiot compassion*. In such a case, we rely
on a shallow and ultimately selfish notion of helping that is
primarily concerned with eliminating our own unease rather
than truly lending a hand. There are numerous simple examples of idiot compassion that beleaguer us at work. The new
receptionist, anxious to contribute, stays late and rearranges
all the supply cabinets, confusing the entire staff for weeks.
The sales rep, wanting to close the sale, not only leaves behind
three pounds of marketing material but also FedExes two addi-
tional sets just to be helpful. The customer service rep, anxious to assist, asks not once but four times, "Is there anything
else I can do to help you today?" Such behavior is common at
work—people trying to be helpful out of nervousness and in
turn making the workday just a bit more difficult for the very
people they are trying to please. Unfortunately, idiot compassion is not limited to well-intentioned but irritating foul-ups.
It can derail careers, ruin friendships, and sink entire businesses.

One of the most common acts of idiot compassion is not
being honest with a subordinate about getting the job done.
How often have we seen poor performers languish for
months—sometimes years—in roles beyond their capabilities?
Managers avoid the stress of telling the truth and instead become defensive and protective of the subordinate. Wanting to
be helpful, the manager protects the employee from the pain

of confronting the problem, and they both avoid the fact that the job is not getting done. As time passes, being honest and straightforward becomes increasingly difficult—tense, uncomfortable, and potentially explosive—and the problem festers. Finally, circumstances demand candor. Confronted with the poor results, the employee spills forth with anger and resentment: "I've never really been supported around here. Every project I've had has been underbudgeted and ultimately shelved. And now you come to me and say I'm to blame!" Bewildered, the manager sees an ungrateful employee rather than a crisis authored by idiot compassion. Instead of confronting the difficulties when they first appeared, the manager chose to avoid the discomfort of being straightforward. The result is a derailed and angry employee and a manager who has learned to dress up guilt and uneasiness as "being helpful." Avoiding idiot compassion encourages us to be honest about our stress—to acknowledge it, feel it, contemplate it. Of course, confronting our subordinate with her marginal performance will be difficult, but to hide from the unease by pretending to be helpful only seals our fate for more damaging problems to come.

When idiot compassion becomes an unspoken rule of leadership, work can become deeply discouraging for hundreds, maybe thousands, of employees. For example, morale problems are singularly complicated and confusing, requiring leaders to be exceptionally skillful in helping the organization reenliven itself. Addressing the hidden problems of poor morale requires patience and openness to criticism, a willingness to listen to the gripe sessions and hear the bad news. Some leaders, in hopes of avoiding such distress, "help" organizations by implementing surefire programs to demonstrate that the company really does care. One particular executive I recall from my years on Wall Street decided to confront head-on the wide-spread belief among operations employees that they were undervalued and were being treated as expendable. Against some others' better judgment, the executive decided to launch an Employee of the Month program, announcing far and wide in posters and newsletters that she valued employees and their contributions. Rather than taking the time to listen carefully to employees' concerns, include them in solving problems, and implement changes that would strengthen morale for the long term—a stressful process indeed—she chose idiot compassion, masking her unease with shallow gestures of help. After four Employees of the Month, the program became widely dismissed as simple favoritism. Employees believed—accurately or not—that those who would not speak their mind or challenge management were getting the recognition because, "just as everyone had known," management valued compliance over the truth. The executive tried other programs—spot bonuses for employees showing extra effort, vacation days for teams exceeding targets—but to no avail. The work environment became increasingly tense and dysfunctional, and the executive became confirmed in her unspoken opinion that the employees were simply ungrateful. Avoiding idiot compassion in this instance required that the executive not look for an easy solution, trying to rescue herself from distressing circumstances. What was required was an experienced helping hand and ear, listening carefully before acting, building trust among managers and subordinates, learning instead of directing. Avoiding idiot compassion suggests that we pause to consider what is truly needed when helping others—that rather than jumping to solutions or rushing to the rescue, we can be discerning and deliberate in our efforts. Especially when circumstances are distressing, "Avoid idiot compassion" reminds us to be slightly suspicious of our need to help. If we are careful, we can linger with our unease and extend a skillful hand of assistance, not one of nervousness masquerading as an easy solution. Avoiding idiot compassion reveals that being helpful has many faces: listening, giving advice, directly solving a problem, speaking candidly—or maybe just going away.

22

Study the six confusions

IF WE ARE GOING to be awake at work, we need to understand how we have fallen asleep to begin with. Exploring this is necessarily very personal. Recognizing our blind spots, our uneasy habits, our hopes and fears, can make us feel exposed and vulnerable. We may feel ashamed of our insecurities and anxieties, consider them mere distractions, or get angry with ourselves for being "weak" and "cowardly." We each work with our anxieties and confusions in our own way. Yet, investigating such confusion need not be an embarrassing or solemn occasion. Examining carefully how we imprison ourselves at work can be a noble act, a candid gesture that can point the way for developing our authenticity on the job.

In Tibetan Buddhism, meditators study the six confusions as one way to understand how we become imprisoned by our lives. The six confusions illustrate how we grasp for certainty in a life that is constantly changing and offering no guarantees. Rather than awaken to the reality that there is nothing to hold on to, we construct a grand self-deception, living a misguided effort to permanently confirm a sense of self—a sense that "I am going to be okay." This effort to be certain about ourselves—that our lives, our jobs, indeed our very existence are somehow guaranteed—is traditionally depicted as a wheel with six spokes spinning around and around in an endless painful struggle called samsara.

At the very core of this struggle is the human fear that life could end or go horribly wrong at any given moment. We become bewildered by this reality and seek assurances that it is otherwise. We mistakenly seek security from our world, surrounding ourselves with the familiar and predictable, struggling to eliminate anything questionable and threatening. Ultimately we become panicky when the enterprise proves useless; we simply cannot avoid death or life's disappointments. In our panic we struggle more, becoming increasingly resentful of our lives and imprisoned by our circumstances.

The wheel of the six confusions depicts a profound irony. It points out that it is in trying to rescue ourselves from life's difficulties that we actually end up imprisoning ourselves in them. The more we try to protect ourselves, the more we become confused. The six confusions are actually six styles or mind-sets that describe how we imprison ourselves at work.

Work as Drudgery

Work as drudgery is the mentality of a beast of burden—stubborn, single-minded, and humorless. We keep our heads down, follow instructions, and put our hands out occasionally for feeding in the form of a paycheck. We shrink from anything that is out of the ordinary or new. We prefer our livelihood to consist of manageable, predictable transactions, so we roll along sticking to the script, ignoring intrusions and alternative possibilities of all kinds. Such an attitude can make us feel dense and unresponsive. The reluctant cashier, the stubborn accountant, the unfriendly police officer all participate in the work-as-drudgery mind-set.

The drudgery mentality secretly wishes to be somewhere else, to get away from work and back to living. We feel work is an impediment to living life rather than an opportunity to do so. We separate livelihood from the rest of our lives: our jobs become a tax we must pay before we can go home. By giving in to this mentality, we become deaf and dumb to our work surroundings, unable to contribute or lend a helping hand. We feel clumsy and somewhat embarrassed by our livelihood, unavailable to see anything outside our need to survive. As beasts of burden, we would just like to keep our blinders on and get back to our stalls, where we can have our lives back.

If we examine the work-as-drudgery mind-set closely, we discover that our burden is not the work but our stubbornness. Our unwillingness to lift our heads up is the real drudgery, not the job itself.

Work as War

Another mind-set we may find ourselves indulging is *work as war*. This is a win-lose mentality. Livelihood makes sense only if we win, because losers are subject to ridicule and shame, and such a position is beneath us. We distill livelihood down to a very simple proposition: everything at work is the enemy unless proven otherwise. We are constantly testing our world: any person, thing, or circumstance that does not further what we need is labeled as foe or, at best, irrelevant. Our every act focuses on eliminating any possibility of failure and ensuring success. We become imprisoned by a constant game of one-upmanship with our work world.

Work as war is a common mind-set: witness win-at-all-costs politicians, Wall Street traders, corporate raiders, divorce lawyers. Such an aggressive approach to work imprisons us in a constant impulse to maintain our point of view. Our entire world must constantly be "dealt with" and controlled. We become trapped in an angry game to protect our version of who we are.

If we examine work-as-war mentality closely, we discover that our war is not with our work but with our own insecurity. Ashamed of our fears and vulnerabilities, we attack our work-world first in order to prevent any possibility of loss or humiliation. Our insecurity is the true enemy, not our work.

Work as Addiction

Work as addiction is a mentality obsessed with overcoming a feeling of inadequacy. Whatever we do at work and however we engage the challenge, it never seems to be enough. So we drive ourselves to do more and more and more. We may find ourselves working eighty-hour weeks, reviewing paperwork and reports on the weekend. We become preoccupied with *thinking* about work, rehearsing issues, and planning ways to complete our tasks. We may find ourselves overpreparing, overengineering our livelihood and workplace activities. We are constantly haunted by a sense that more has to be done.

The work-as-addiction mind-set is unnerved by obstacles and gaps. "Incompetent" people, computer glitches, broken pencils—anything that prevents us from completing the job—frustrate us and at times drive us into a frenzy. As workaholics, we may be perfectionists, up every morning at exactly the right time; sharp, reliable at work, and proud of our high standards. Praise from the boss or a colleague thrills us, but such satisfaction is fleeting and never enough. We find ourselves in a cycle of frustration again and again—unfulfilled, yet willing to sacrifice our lives in our addiction to work.

If we examine our addiction closely, we discover that we are not addicted to work but are paralyzed by our own sense of poverty, frozen in a pattern of frustration over our many desires left unfulfilled. Work becomes an anesthesia—a drug for numbing us to our pain.

Work as Entertainment

The mentality of *work as entertainment* is based on our suspicion that we are going to miss out on all the fun. We look around at work and see others looking good, laughing, and having a wonderful time of it, and we suspect that we may have missed the boat. Others are getting promotions, flying off to sales meetings in the Bahamas, wearing fashionable new clothes, attending important meetings where you get free Danish pastries. Other people seem to have mastered their work world, and we suspect that we are out of step. We too want to win access to work's amusements and pleasures; we want the prestige and free Danish.

As we develop our work-as-entertainment mentality, we look to work as a source of amusement and leisure. We learn to become masters of showmanship, displaying our successes and power and conveniences—with restraint, of course, but conspicuously enough to garner attention. We amass conveniences like toys, acquiring buttons to push anywhere and anytime—home, car, office, and plane—that make stuff happen. Our jobs become a kind of game or recreation. We come to believe that we are entitled to these conveniences, that we are very much deserving of our status and pleasures.

For work to be entertaining, untidiness generally needs to be kept out of sight, so we become expert at packaging bad news and nuisances. We learn to enlist others in making work appear neat and manageable. Secretaries, subordinates, accounting and consulting firms, even charities are all seen as ways to smooth over work's difficulties. We expect our world to be neat and predictable, and insist—usually through someone else—that our expectations be met, and we sit back and enjoy the packaged results. The work-as-entertainment mentality is as much about ignoring work as indulging its pleasures and prestige.

Government capitals, universities, corporate boardrooms, and executive suites throughout the world are crowded with this mind-set. But such lofty imprisonment is not reserved for grand institutions. It can just as easily happen at the traffic court or the lumberyard. Being imprisoned by our fascination with power, prestige, or position can be orchestrated from the most mundane or most regal of stations. If we were to examine the work-as-entertainment mentality closely, we would discover that we are not actually savoring life's pleasures but have become trapped in an uninterrupted, sugarcoated vacation from reality—unable even to know there is anything more to life than amassing toys and indulging pleasures.

Work as Inconvenience

The mind-set of *work as inconvenience* assumes that the need to make a living is some kind of unfortunate accident that has happened to us. We should not be sullied by work's many difficulties. We are deserving of so much more. We are entitled to a life that runs smoothly, and all the messiness of work—managing conflicts, fixing problems, making the "trains run on time"—is such an imposition, something that is beneath us.

We envision ourselves as an artist or poet or organic gardener; earning a paycheck is a distasteful distraction from such greatness. We need to devote ourselves to larger issues such as coloring our canvas or speaking our mind. Or we may be a successful executive or doctor or professor who is asked to sit on the board of a charity to help the homeless—appropriate given our know-how and wisdom—but we first want to be sure that such a venture is equal to our station in life. Maybe the governor has signed a slip of paper saying it was an important charity, or maybe a famous movie star had attended a meeting or two in the past and pictures were taken with other board members. That kind of charity work would not be inconvenient, since we are deserving of such lofty acknowledgments.

The work-as-inconvenience mentality is defensive and prideful, constantly on guard for the possibility of being victimized by work's circumstances. It is paranoid and continually concerned about getting the wrong end of the stick. We are always comparing our fate and position with others' and feeling cheated. Distrustful of what we are seeing and hearing, we begin to filter the messages we get from our work world, ignoring feedback that doesn't fit our exalted view of ourselves.

If we closely examine such a mentality, we discover that it is not work that is inconvenient but our nagging sense of entitlement that is so tiresome. It is our fear of being victimized that is inconvenient, not work itself.

Work as a Problem

Work as a problem assumes that we need to *solve* work—to get work to behave and stop being so unpredictable and unruly. We know that work could behave logically if only things would get back on track—and we are just the one to do it! Such a mind-set is idealistic and oddly naive. We are convinced there is a best solution, a just or right way of going about our jobs, and we aspire to make such an important contribution.

This mentality is constantly ambitious, always searching for the new technique or strategy. "If everyone would just follow the advice in this little book, *Who Stole My Baloney?* we would finally be able to make sense of our work problems and would all be more easygoing." Or maybe meditation will solve the problem, relieve our stress and get our jobs back to the way they're supposed to be—fun, creative, and smooth sailing. In our hearts we want to make a heroic contribution, one worthy of praise and recognition. We may admire someone at work who actually meditates or lives everything taught in *Who Stole My Baloney?* We want to be just like that person. Those who seem to be missing the *Baloney* boat become irritating and disappointing to us. The work-as-a-problem mind-set is convinced that work is fundamentally a logical exercise, and such things as human conflict, errors in judgment, common mistakes, emotions—all of work's unruly and messy aspects—can be "fixed" if we learn the right lessons, apply the right techniques, and gather the right information.

If we were to examine this mentality, we would discover that work is not the problem. Our ambition and constant busyness attempting to solve work turn out to be the problem, not work, which will always be unruly and messy.

By studying the six confusions, we may notice aspects of ourselves. Maybe we are addicted to our work, overly involved, unable to keep our jobs in perspective. Or maybe we are resentful of our jobs and work has become simple drudgery. We may find that under stress we tend to be arrogant and aggres-sive—the work-as-war mentality. Aspects of all six mentalities may seem to arise and fade depending upon circumstances. By contemplating and studying the six confusions more and more, we begin to see our insecure patterns and better under-stand how we imprison ourselves at work. The more we learn, the more we ask: "How do I get out of the cycle? How do I stop imprisoning myself?"

Studying the six confusions alone cannot free us from the fears and anxieties that imprison us at work. Developing bal-anced effort, touching our inherent sense of authenticity, dropping our bias, and much more is required if we are going to overcome the ordeals of the six confusions. Yet, recognizing that *we, not work*, are imprisoning ourselves is critical if we expect to rediscover well-being in our livelihoods. Our anger, impoverishment, and sense of entitlement are the bars of our prison at work; they are the burdens that wear us down, keep-ing us anxious and fearful of what might happen. Studying the six confusions invites us to examine this powerful fact of work life. We need not blame our jobs, our colleagues, or our work circumstances for our confusion. Nor do we need to blame ourselves. We do, however, need to take a sobering look at how our struggles to protect ourselves from work's difficulties imprison us over and over and over again.

23

Extend the four composures

IT IS A GREAT IRONY that we make our awake-at-work journey by learning to sit still. Nonetheless, taking such a posture is the fundamental act of well-being that we offer to ourselves and others throughout the journey. By sitting upright with our senses fully alert and attending gently and precisely to our breath, we cultivate a simple and powerful wakefulness that is sane, open, and free. Scientific studies have documented many of the physical and psychological benefits to sitting meditation: lower blood pressure, increased brain patterns associated with feelings of joy, reduced anxiety, and heightened alertness to one's surroundings. While such benefits can be quite helpful, it is not why Eastern traditions consider meditation a worthy activity. Buddhists regard the very act of sitting itself as the ultimate expression of human decency and poise. Having the composure to sit down and be still is considered utterly dignified and profoundly human. Such composure is in fact our authenticity—our basic confidence in ourselves that we are not trapped by our lives but free to live them.

When we are awake at work, we extend this composure into

our job, our career, and our entire livelihood. In fact, sitting provides us the opportunity to extend the four composures into our work, guiding us to be more effective at our jobs and more helpful to others.

The Composure of Kindness

In sitting, when we come back to the present moment, we drop our preoccupation with our point of view and story lines over and over again. At first this may seem a struggle, but over time it can become a great relief. Our anger with a colleague, our stubbornness over a business deal, our defensiveness over a slip of the tongue—all can be dropped, if only for a brief moment. At once this creates space and room to breathe and be. Such a gesture toward ourselves is traditionally considered an act of kindness, giving ourselves a break, so to speak. When we think of being kind, we usually think of petting a kitten or giving someone who is in need of money a ten-dollar bill. Here we are being kind in a different manner: we are being kind to ourselves by dropping the burden of maintaining our preconceptions. By practicing this in meditation, we learn that we can have the same composure at work, dropping our fixed views of our colleagues and making a gracious and kind gesture, giving *them* a break, giving them space and room to be. The kindness we extend to ourselves in meditation, we can now extend to others at work.

The Composure of Respecting Difficulties

In sitting we don't just concentrate on developing our clarity of mind or sharpness of purpose; we also recognize our confusion, arrogance, and fear. By sitting still, we get to know ourselves directly and learn, over time, to respect and acknowledge not just our strengths but our seeming weaknesses as well. They are not inconveniences or sins to be eliminated from our lives. We need not resent or dismiss our jealousies or insecurities as mistakes we should be ashamed of. By sitting still with ourselves, we learn to respect and attend to our "negativities" rather than resist and argue with them, to explore and unravel them rather than throw them away. In doing so, we engender a wise and gentle humanity that we can bring to the job. We gradually develop a composure at work where we learn to respect work's messiness and difficulties, not resist them.

The Composure of Calm Alertness

When we sit for any period of time, we inevitably notice that we are bored. We are doing nothing, just sitting there. Our culture would have us believe that something must be wrong if we are bored. There must be a problem, since we're not achieving anything. Maybe we are not up to the task at hand. We should get back to work. When we are bored, we normally look for something else to do, maybe watch TV or play a game or eat. "Do something!" We do anything—play digital games on our cell phones, doodle on the back of our hands, *anything*—just to keep from being bored.

In sitting we develop a composure that takes the exact opposite view. By bringing our attention back to the moment over and over again, we make friends with boredom and notice that we can be powerfully alert in the immediate moment without need for distractions or entertainment of any kind. Over time we become comfortable being in the moment. We develop a "calm alertness" that becomes central to relating directly to our work, giving us perspective and precision, an ability to engage work on its terms as it unfolds moment by moment. We can also extend this calm alertness we develop in sitting to the challenges of our job.

The Composure of Availability

Generally we apply effort in order to achieve something. Especially at work, we strive to accomplish goals and realize rewards; we work for results. Such effort is forward looking and determined and is central to achieving our goals at work. In sitting, however, we learn to apply an effort that is not seeking results but is the effort of being in the present moment. We learn to let go of rehashing the past and rehearsing for the future. In meditation, when we notice that we are lost in thoughts, we bring our attention back to the present moment. We let go of our preoccupations; we let go of our "story lines" and versions and leap into the present moment with no guarantees or viewpoints. Whatever arises in meditation, we are gently available to, open and attentive. This availability we develop in meditation, when extended to the workplace, permits us to be open to our work setting and colleagues, attentive to what the situation requires.

The slogan "Extend the four composures" encourages us to cultivate a sitting meditation practice as a way of reinventing and uplifting our lives at work. The appendix "Instructions for Mindfulness-Awareness Meditation" offers meditation instruction for those who may be new to meditation and would like to get started. By developing a sitting practice, we can unfold a natural dignity and poise in our jobs. We can show to others the kindness we show to ourselves in meditation. We can extend the respect we show for our seeming shortcomings and negativities to work's messiness as well. The calm alertness we develop in meditation by resting in the uncontrived moment can be extended to the challenges of the job. Our willingness to be attentive and available to whatever arises in our sitting—that too can be extended to our colleagues at work. Extending the four composures reminds us that we are not sitting for our own sake alone but in order to be more helpful to others and effective while being awake at work.

24

Everybody just wants to bounce their ball

IN MY SENIOR YEAR of high school a German priest taught
me and my classmates how to think. For a year we studied
Aristotelian logic, the Socratic method, John Stuart Mill's
Utilitarianism, syllogistic reasoning, logical fallacies, deductive
and inductive reasoning, a priori and a posteriori statements.
We also analyzed advertisements and listened to political
speeches in order to recognize deception, and we debated
points of view, listened carefully to each other's arguments,
and sharpened our intellects through endless exercises in rational thinking. We were trained well in analyzing life's situations logically, systematically, rationally.

As final exams drew near, our teacher began to take a much
different approach to our training. Rather than questioning
definitions of terms or insisting on a more concise analysis of
a particular newspaper article, he began to pull the rug out
from under our feet in a profound but at the time barely no-
ticeable way. We spent two classes trying to understand why

people laugh, for example. Or he would have us discuss "Why does a mother love her child?" Survival of the fittest, we would conclude, of course. But there was no logic to explain the tenderness or sadness of a mother; there was no rationality to a punch line.

On our final class together with this wise and gentle man—a day I will always remember and cherish—he gave us a little speech that I recall to this very day.

When we started off the year, many of you gentle-men felt that learning to think was rather silly. Some said to me, "We all think, so what's there to learn?" But now, after a year, you see that thinking properly is demanding. To think properly is to be responsible and honest. To think properly is to be disciplined and to listen well. To think properly, in the end, is to be logical.

Yet, gentlemen, I leave you with one last lesson— probably the most important lesson I have to offer. Life, my dear fellows, is not logical. While you may work hard throughout your lives to be fair and rea-sonable, thorough and correct, your lives will not follow such rules. And if you try to understand your fellow human beings by logic alone, you will be doing yourselves and others a great disservice. There is actually something much more basic and important that is at the heart of every human being.

Our teacher began to walk around the classroom, placing a single sheet of paper facedown on each of our desks.

So I leave you today with one final puzzle that I hope you keep with you for the rest of your lives. Contemplate it, remember it, let its meaning unfold. I believe that what I am handing you will be helpful to you in understanding what we all really want as human beings.

I turned the sheet of paper over to discover a rather unremarkable photograph from a local newspaper. It was a picture of a young boy standing alone outside an empty basketball court. The shot was taken from behind him. He had a basketball under one arm and gripped the tall chain-link fence with his free hand. Though it was a warm, sunny day, the court was empty and the gate was locked. The caption below read "Everybody just wants to bounce their ball."

Our teacher had timed his speech perfectly, for at that moment the bell rang and there was no time for questions or discussion. He simply said farewell and good luck.

My first reaction to my teacher's final speech and his picture of a kid wanting to play basketball was that it was kind of silly and trite, given the significance of what he had taught us throughout the year. For many years I rarely thought of that final speech and captioned photograph. But eventually it did haunt me and drew me back to contemplate why he had chosen such a picture. Why was the boy fenced out on a sunny day? Who was the boy? Why would a basketball court be locked?

Ultimately, after fifteen years, the riddle finally revealed its secret—a deeply personal lesson on how to conduct myself in business and in life. And though these are not my teacher's actual words, I can hear them in my heart today as if they were being spoken from his lips to my ears:

Don't take yourselves so seriously, gentlemen, for if you do, you will miss what it means to be human. Your logic and correctness, your rationality and thoroughness, can actually blind you, lock you out of the game, prevent you from becoming who you most deeply want to be.

"Everybody just wants to bounce their ball" reminds us to respect the gentle enthusiasm that everyone brings to life. All of us want to do our best and have a chance to contribute and shine. All of us want to leave behind something to be proud of and to be remembered as an inspiring person. Whether we are a gardener or a CEO, an engineer or a housepainter; whether we are knitting pot holders or curing cancer, we all want to make life better for others and show what we can do. We were all children once, wanting to be our best.

And if in our quest to succeed—in our drive to be profitable, powerful, and secure—we forget that everyone just wants to bounce their ball, we most likely will find ourselves standing on the outside, imprisoned by the fence of our logic and correctness, unable to live our lives properly; unable to bounce *our* ball.

25

Treat everyone as a guest

FOR A MOMENT, think back five or six years, maybe more, and recall a colleague or two who made your work life colorful and enjoyable. Maybe a kindhearted cafeteria worker comes to mind, or the trusted executive who supported your work on the most satisfying project of your career, or a wacky coworker who always had a hilarious insight to share. As you think back and paint a mental picture of these people, you will probably recall some warm and cherished times you spent with them. You had extended yourself to these colleagues—been open and available—and the camaraderie had made some aspect of your life at work fulfilling.

Chances are the people we are recalling are no longer a part of our lives. If we are lucky, we may have remained in contact with some of our work friends. But more often we find that the people we appreciated have moved on: perhaps they have taken new jobs elsewhere, or maybe just moved to New Zealand. It may be disheartening to realize that our relationships at work are so fleeting. But by recognizing that work's relationships are fluid and constantly changing, we can actually enliven and

cultivate the very collegial warmth that we so value. Colleagues come and go—new faces, unexpected reunions, new
team members. This shifting landscape of work relationships
invites us to deliberately appreciate our colleagues in the immediate moment, to be gracious and accessible at work—to
"treat everyone as a guest."

Normally when we treat someone as a guest, we acknowledge in everything we do that our time together is rare and
worthy of our appreciation. We do not just serve any meal or
offer the person sloppy hospitality. When a guest arrives, we
do not treat her as an inconvenience, pointing her to the refrigerator, where she can find leftovers. On the contrary, we
naturally work hard to be cordial and available, and we extend
to our guest our very finest. As truly gracious hosts, we extend
that invitation openly; we do not favor one guest over another. When we have a dinner party and guests arrive that we
have not met before, we do not say, "Well, these are new people so give them the cheap wine or serve them with paper
plates." If anything, we may extend extra care to such guests.
Even if we have a guest that we do not necessarily get along
with, we do not rush up and say, "Excuse me, you are not my
type of guest. Please leave by the back door." Whether our
guests are strangers or best friends, neighbors or passing travelers, cheerful newcomers or cranky diehards, we instinctively
extend to them open and appealing hospitality that acknowledges that our time together is rare and worthwhile.

In the same way, "Treat everyone as a guest" encourages us
to rely on our natural instincts to treat others properly and
graciously, respecting our work relationships by being genuinely available to others and extending our very finest to
everyone we meet. When we present an idea or opinion, we
serve it properly so others can appreciate and digest what we

are saying. We do not discriminate among our colleagues. Whether it's the CEO or the custodian, we are considerate and cordial to all. When we go to work, we dress properly and precisely, so we can communicate a sense of cheerfulness and wholesomeness. When others have a point of view, we listen carefully; we "cultivate the art of conversation." Even when our colleagues are offensive or inconsiderate, we can remain courteous, promoting decency by cultivating *li*. We do such things not as some kind of mindless servant who wants to please everyone or out of a sense of neediness. We treat everyone as a guest because we are naturally dignified. Confident, curious, and resourceful, we can extend enormous space and well-being toward others, even under tough circumstances, because it is quite simply the authentic thing to do—a natural expression of who we are.

When we treat everyone as a guest, we offer tremendous breathing room, permitting everyone we meet to be who they are, where they are, in that very moment. As hosts at a dinner party, we encourage our guests to freely and cheerfully express themselves; we do the same at work. Rather than trying to control our work circumstances, we allow ourselves the freedom to appreciate our colleagues and "not know," letting those we encounter be who they are without our preconceptions and bias. From such a vantage point, we can appreciate our colleagues' individual concerns, styles, foibles, and talents.

Because we are not impoverished or intimidated by our work circumstances, we can afford to provide our guests our finest. Thus, treating everyone as a guest continually inspires us to engage and appreciate each valuable and authentic moment. More important, it reminds us to extend to each colleague a deep sense of gratitude. For we are actually deeply indebted to everyone we meet, to all our guests at work. If we look carefully at work relationships, we will discover that our colleagues have taught us some of the most important lessons we need in order to be awake at work. Allies and adversaries, competitors and supporters, strangers and friends alike, all give us endless opportunities to drop our arrogance, neediness, and fear and be authentic. Such guests, who invite us to be genuinely who we are, naturally deserve only the best.

26

Witness from the heart

AT WORK WE inevitably experience other people's conflicts, struggles, and misfortunes. Maybe a colleague fails in his job, becomes resentful toward his manager, and grows sullen and withdrawn. Perhaps team members are at odds with one another, blaming one another for perceived mistakes and failures. Or maybe a manager seems condescending to her subordinates, who then gossip that she is arrogant, a poor leader, and afraid of her job.

When we see others troubled or quarreling at work, we may want to help. Because we are basically decent—because we possess *li*—we naturally want to relieve people's misfortune. Helping others resolve conflicts or manage disappointments is never as easy as it may seem. We may be part of the conflict ourselves. There is always a potential blind spot of idiot compassion that can derail our efforts to help. Yet we can appreciate and better understand disagreements and difficulties at work by learning to witness from the heart.

Witnessing from the heart begins with our experience of witnessing ourselves in sitting meditation. When we sit, we allow ourselves to witness our minds, and we give ourselves enormous space. We may witness our worry and insecurity or our speediness and restlessness. Or we may witness the vastness of being alive or the cool boredom of being sharply present, moment by moment. We watch our minds race, then slow. We watch our breath rise and fall. Such mindfulness, such willingness to let ourselves be who we are, where we are, is the basis for witnessing from the heart at work. Such mindfulness prepares us to gently witness conflicts, quarrels, and distress as they unfold, just as we witness our lives unfold when we sit on the cushion, with no filters: alert, open, and available.

This approach to workplace difficulties is not a way to remain detached, like a disinterested observer or benevolent tour guide. Rather, such mindfulness permits the difficulties to be exactly what they are, uncontaminated with our agendas and our versions. Fully appreciating the problem—not ignoring it, arguing with it, fixing it, or sugarcoating the difficult parts—is an essential gesture of openness. We take no sides nor grind any ax. We witness the difficulty without bias or preconceptions.

Workplace struggles can be quite disturbing and personally penetrating when we're open to them in such a way because we are getting a straight dose of the distress. While such an approach may give us a clear picture as the situation unfolds, we inevitably will also notice that we are sad. We're not sad in an anxious or depressed way: "Oh, it's so awful that Mary is refusing to work with Bill." Nor are we sad because we pity our colleague's fate: "Poor Jim, he's such a loser that he once again lost the sale. I feel sorry for him." The sadness we experience in witnessing from the heart is because we have actually touched our colleagues' distress, because we are fully engaged in the emotions of the moment.

Such sadness is a very physical feeling, a kind of tenderness or openness we feel in our chest or stomach. Some of us call it "having a heart." When we feel such sadness—when we have a heart at work—we may want to move away from such poignant feelings. We may think to ourselves, "This is business. There is no room for getting emotional about other people's difficulties. We should be efficient about such things—assess the problem, propose a solution, and move on. There's work to be done." Such a rational approach to conflicts and difficulties has its virtues, no doubt. But when we witness from the heart, we are taking a large view. Rather than avoiding this sadness because it seems unproductive, we actually make friends with it. We include it as part of engaging the problem. By doing so, we gradually learn that such sadness is not weak or "emotional" but unshakable and clear seeing. When we permit ourselves to "have a heart"—to be open and to touch another's distress directly, we discover a single-minded wisdom that is unafraid of not knowing, leaving us open to being helpful without feeling a need to rescue anybody.

Witnessing from the heart reminds us that being heartbroken by our colleagues' difficulties is our natural instinct, inviting us to see and act clearly. When we witness from the heart as a colleague struggles with being fired, we also see the whole picture—that it is actually time for him to move on, to refresh his view of himself and adapt. When we witness from the heart as coworkers gossip about someone, we also see that they are destroying themselves with cowardice, and when we eventually take the time to confront the gossip, we do so precisely and firmly. Or, as a colleague angrily replays her resentment about being transferred off a project, when we witness from the heart we sense that we must simply listen.

Witnessing from the heart reminds us that we can rely on our hearts at work, that there is no embarrassment to our sadness. When we see others struggle or experience misfortune, we can lead with our heart because there is strength and wisdom in such tenderness. Just as we give ourselves room on the cushion to experience ourselves fully, we can extend such openness of heart to others in distress. By doing so we can learn to be genuinely helpful from a wise and skillful place.

PART FOUR

ACTING PRECISELY

The nine slogans in this section point out that we can perform our jobs in the immediate moment without guarantees or confirmations while gently and powerfully experiencing "awake mind."

- Don't forget
- Appreciate the intimacy of morning routines
- Acknowledge small boredoms
- Respect karma
- Do not-know
- Be humble while ambitious
- Notice and cut work's speed
- Take a fresh glimpse and adapt
- Keep your seat

When we mix these slogans with our daily work, we are challenged to wake up on the spot. If we are brave enough to drop our resistance and remain open to work as it unfolds moment by moment, we inevitably face the profound reality of simply being alive—remarkably, vividly, and vastly on the spot in the immediate moment. Acknowledging this reality—glimpsing it at first, feeling its ever-present rhythm, then befriending its frequent visits—is not alien to work; it is what our jobs have been inviting us to embrace all along. The nine slogans in this section point out that experiencing awake mind as a part of our daily work not only is unavoidable but is the key to the success we have been looking for.

27

Don't forget

AT TIMES IT SEEMS impossible to escape our impatience. The overnight Federal Express package isn't express enough; our 900 million mega-RAM computer boots up too slowly; the thirty-second wait at the elevator, the sorting time at the copier, the line at the toll booth—our anger and impatience at waiting and our resistance to slowing down can seem monumental. It is little wonder that our patience is thin, however. Our consumer society markets speed and efficiency as a virtual human entitlement: fast food, one-hour photos, overnight mail, channel surfing, instant messaging, sound bites, speed-dialing. We construct our world for convenience and then end up feeling impatient and frustrated when we can't speed past the present moment. Such entitlement leads to intolerance and the need for instant gratification.

Hundreds of studies and books have cataloged the biology of impatience: stress, high blood pressure, road rage, heart disease, chronic fatigue, substance abuse. Much inspiring advice is offered: take a moment to relax each day, get exercise, watch the sugar intake, count to ten, spend time with loved ones, take a deep breath. Yet it seems hard to take the advice when it is most needed. In the midst of the pressing panic and speed and annoyance, we forget to breathe, we forget to relax, we forget our loved ones, and we forget to slow down. In fact, we forget to wake up. We lose touch with our ability to live a meaningful and useful life.

When we are awake at work, we don't forget to wake up; we can do this because we practice mindfulness meditation. Of course, even if we become the greatest, most accomplished meditator, we will still lose our patience at times—there are never guarantees. But when we mix our impatience with mindfulness, we don't forget that being who we are where we are is utterly and perfectly sufficient. We are constantly reminded of the simple reality of our authenticity. The traffic jam is intolerable, but we don't forget to notice the bumper sticker "Dear God, save us from those who believe in you," and we laugh. The project manager is livid—we've missed the deadline, we're over budget, and two people are late for the meeting—but we don't forget to offer our colleague a glass of water. The television is blaring, the phone is ringing, we're typing our final e-mail, and our husband yells, "Dinner's ready," and then, right there, on the spot, we don't forget to wake up.

Normally when we are impatient, we have lost interest in our experience. For whatever reason, being in the present moment seems inadequate. We want to rush on to somewhere else; we want to forget, disregard, or eliminate our irritation. We simply want the present moment to go away. Children twitch their computer games; teenagers surf the TV channels; commuters drive through for fast food; reporters chatter in sound bites; executives rush from meeting to meeting. This impatience to *get somewhere else* rather than be where we are has become a vast and disastrous addiction to forgetfulness. We forget to be who we are; we forget to appreciate our world; we forget to work with life properly and precisely; we forget to help. This addiction to forgetfulness prevents us from experiencing the delight and satisfaction of working with our world with our total being.

As with most addictions, "detoxing" may be required, and mindfulness meditation is our detox program. In sitting meditation we experience the crudeness of our impatience. We sit on our cushion, arrange ourselves properly, and just sit. We attend to our breath, and time passes. Then we begin to feel a bit claustrophobic: "What's next?" we think. "How long do I need to sit here?" We are so bored—no newspapers to read, no e-mail or phone calls, no dinners to eat, no entertainment of any kind. We want to forget that we are here and hurry on, but our mindfulness permits no escape from the present moment. We sit and don't forget and begin to experience the "hot patience" of detoxing. We feel our irritation and discomfort with simply being in the immediate moment, and we want to get away. Maybe we get up and go to the refrigerator or flick on the TV; we take a little vacation, but then we don't forget that we are still with ourselves and we go back to the cushion and we persist. Not forgetting begins with detoxing from our impatience with reality, and it happens quite directly on the cushion.

If we are brave and keep sitting—for hours, weeks, months, and years—our "detox program" unfolds. Our hot patience gradually, gently becomes cool patience, and our addiction to forgetfulness eases up. We begin to think on occasion, "Hey, sitting still isn't so bad after all." We may still get irritated or panicky, but we don't forget to come back to the present moment, and we find our impatience transforming into a simple

165

unshakable composure. In the Hindu and Buddhist traditions, such cool, composed patience has been called the walk of the elephant. Each elephant step is thorough and utterly present. There is no hesitation or questioning. The elephant isn't searching his pockets for a speed-dial cell phone or glancing at his watch as he waits in line to buy a predigested burger. The elephant's cool patience is tough, reliable, and composed. And because of such patience, the elephant never forgets to wake up.

"Don't forget" encourages us to become thoroughly soaked in the cool patience of mindfulness. Rather than rushing, we can be suddenly and sharply mindful on the spot. Because we are mindful, we don't forget to take a deep breath or a sip of water or enjoy a walk in the park. Because we are mindful, we don't forget to be available, to listen deeply, to be patient. We may feel a tinge of impatience as the old woman slowly counts her change at the checkout counter, but then we don't forget to pause and rest in our elephant-like authenticity. There is tremendous delight in working with our world properly and mindfully. "Don't forget" reminds us that we can break the addiction of impatience and remember to be in our world without rushing past the present moment.

28

*Appreciate the intimacy
of morning routines*

MEN AND WOMEN throughout the world rise each morning
and quietly prepare for work. The farmer considers the timing
of a harvest during his familiar morning stroll to the barn; a
mother quietly arranges fresh clothes a few minutes before her
children awake for school; the truck driver enjoys his cup of
coffee as he checks the tires and rigging; the New York banker
breathes deeply of the Hudson River mist while jogging at
dawn. Mornings offer many of us a quiet pause as the day begins, a natural time to feel the texture of our lives and contemplate our workday ahead.

In the quiet of morning, we are naturally relaxed. For just a
moment, we allow some space in our lives. Bathing, dressing,
sipping a cup of tea, walking the dog, walking to the train
station, are all quiet, simple habits, soothing and uplifting.
We are alone in these moments, brief as they may be; just
ourselves, with our life unfolding once again. Our day ahead
may hand us significant responsibilities, such as running a

government or a classroom; we may have exacting tasks to accomplish, such as repairing a wounded heart or a damaged bridge. But before we engage the sheer size of it all once again, we are alone with ourselves, being kind to ourselves in some simple way.

In our hurried pace, we may rush past such ordinary, quiet moments. Maybe our nine-person family shares one bathroom and we spend our mornings urging others to hurry up. Maybe we like to sleep late and leave ourselves time only for a frantic dash to a train or car pool. Kids to school, e-mail to be checked, cell phones ringing before we even get out of the house. Such hectic demands can invade our morning's quiet pause and hijack the intimacy of our routines, launching us into our daily work rushed and distracted. Yet even then, even when our franticness seems so large and intrusive, mornings still haunt us and invite us to slow down, let go for just a moment.

Appreciating the intimacy of morning routines encourages us to accept our mornings' invitations to linger with the quiet moment and allow some gentle space into our lives. We could treat our mornings as a daily practice, a deliberate time for spiritual reflection and meditation. Morning meditation is a time-honored Buddhist way to show respect for ourselves and our lives. Each morning, in Buddhist homes and communities throughout the world, the day begins with a moment of meditation. Shrine candles and incense sticks are lit. Tea is offered. Some chant the *Heart Sutra*, others simply sit. Throughout Tibet, before launching into life's daily labors, men, women, and children rise with the dawn to circumambulate the local stupa, or temple, gently reciting mantras and reflecting on life's meaning. City parks in Chinatowns throughout the United States are the early-morning shrine rooms for thousands practicing tai chi. Zen monks in Japan begin their day at 4:00 a.m. sitting *zazen* and eating breakfast silently in *oryoki*. Whether we choose to sit meditation each morning, sip our coffee mindfully, or start our day with some other gesture of gentle ease, deliberately appreciating our lives can be a profoundly wholesome act.

By appreciating the intimacy of morning routines, we begin our day expressing a very basic confidence: that we are comfortable being who we are, as we are. Our morning routines may feel lonely yet heartfelt, simple and quiet yet alert and fresh. This is the intimacy that we savor: we enjoy being exactly who we are for a brief moment, confident in simply being ourselves. We need not rush past such moments, gulping down our breakfast or distracting ourselves with radio talk-show updates. We can pause and fully appreciate our lives on the spot.

Appreciating the intimacy of morning routines suggests that our experience of who we are in the quiet of morning— before we hurry, before we begin our hectic day—lets us glimpse our basic authenticity, an intimate moment of simply being. We may run the UN or just a lemonade stand; we may be a famous artist or a toll collector in Tennessee, but in the end we are all utterly human *first*. And it is here, in the morning, that we begin everything once again.

29

Acknowledge small boredoms

ALL OF US experience small boredoms at work—routine, seemingly dull events that we often take for granted: remaining "on hold" on the phone, waiting at the copier or coffee line, pausing for a computer screen to open, being stopped in traffic. We may consider such moments irritating or unproductive, a waste of our time to be avoided if possible. However, properly handled, such small boredoms can ease the speed and restlessness of our jobs, helping us remain alert, available, and awake at work.

A common small boredom for many of us is traveling in an elevator. We press the button and wait a moment or two while other passengers assemble for the brief trip. When the doors open, we pause while passengers exit, then slowly file into the small space, selecting our destination and taking our place among our fellow passengers. The doors close and a familiar yet peculiar experience occurs. If we are paying attention, we might notice two things. First, during those few seconds in the elevator, our physical circumstances seem quite immediate. We are close to the elevator walls and to our fellow passengers, with little to see, hear, and smell. Our senses seem unusually keen and our surroundings distinctly vivid. The second thing we might notice is that this immediacy makes us slightly uncomfortable. We quickly begin to do little things to distract ourselves: we shift our weight from foot to foot, glance mechanically at our watch, check the floor numbers, and then glance at our watch again. What is so powerful about the small boredom of the elevator—indeed, about small boredoms in general—is that we are actually *awake* at those routine moments—*but also trying to avoid our experience,* to distract ourselves from the sharp immediacy of the moment.

Small boredoms—whether they are elevator rides, pauses in a speech, or sitting in a traffic jam—can feel vaguely unnerving. We are being poked by our world, provoked, invited to wake up. Acknowledging small boredoms encourages us to engage that slight discomfort by being alert and fully present with no mindless distractions. Rather than letting boredom, short or prolonged, put us to sleep, we reverse the equation, engaging boredom in all its simple, unadorned vividness, letting it wake us up. By relating to small boredoms with this kind of precision, we turn them into practice, stepping-stones we walk each day that form the basis for slowing our speed, letting go of our inner rehearsals, and being fully alert to our circumstances.

A common experience in my corporate career was attending meetings in the boardroom. Over the years, the tone and pace of those meetings varied widely—sometimes tense, other times enjoyable; sometimes hurried, other times measured. No matter what the tone or pace, no matter what the topic or difficulty being discussed, there was always a small boredom that reminded me to be alert, available, and curious.

More often than not, before the meeting could begin, my

colleagues and I would wait in silence for about sixty seconds as conference calls were placed to bring people into the meeting. It was a routine moment, dull and vaguely irritating and uncomfortable. Some would shuffle through their papers or move their pen about on the table. Others would glance out the window or at their watches. The brief pause was a small boredom for me where I would often drop my rehearsals and anxieties and, for a moment, thoroughly relax and notice my surroundings. In the middle of the boardroom table was a speakerphone used for conducting the conference calls. Sitting prominently on the table with its keypad and open speaker design, the device was slightly dented and the numbers on some of the keypads were worn and faded. Over the years I got to know it quite well. In time the speaker by itself represented for me an invitation to cut the speed of my mind, drop my rehearsals, and be present. Eventually just seeing the speakerphone reminded me to wake up. To this day, whenever I see the same model phone, I can't help but be alert and curious about my surroundings.

Acknowledging small boredoms has a peculiar way of permeating and informing our work experience, inviting more and more aspects of our physical setting to poke us and wake us up. The familiar landscape painting that we see each morning as we exit our small boredom in the elevator invites us time and again to wake up. Our coffee mug, in hand as we wait for the coffee to brew, pokes us throughout the day. The worn metal post at our train stop that greets and awakens us each morning now greets and awakens us on our way home at night. Our favorite tie or scarf, the view from our office window, our computer keypad—all invite and provoke us to be awake at work. As we extend our experience of small boredoms, our entire work setting becomes a greater invitation to wake up.

Eventually we begin to feel at home at work. Not in the sense that we can kick off our shoes and walk around in our robe and slippers. Rather, our familiar routines and work settings become a continuous reminder that our world is at once vast and profound yet highly personal and routine. We gradually begin to appreciate the natural pace of our every act: holding a door for a colleague or closing a million-dollar deal, handling a pen or pencil or handing medicine to a dying patient. Surprisingly, by being precise with small boredoms, we discover a way for being precise with work overall. Acknowledging small boredoms reminds us that we need not be numbed by work's pressures or routines. By taking the time to notice the seemingly insignificant moments that invite us to wake up, we can, over time, rediscover a natural and precise pace that can inform and uplift all that we do throughout the day.

30

Respect karma

THERE ARE MANY common notions of karma: "Everybody gets what they deserve in the end" or "Play the cards you're dealt" or "Be careful what you wish for." Such ideas actually touch on profound aspects of karma that are indeed worthy of our attention. Yet if we are to actually respect karma as part of being awake at work, we will need to go beyond just a popular understanding.

In its simplest definition, karma is the law of cause and effect governing human behavior. Philosophers, ethicists, psychologists, and teachers throughout the centuries have confronted many of the questions presented by such a notion: If we are governed by cause and effect, are we then predestined? Do we have free will? How should we conduct ourselves in our lives if we are already fated to live out our karma? Why do immoral people often seem to live fruitful lives while decent people live in misery? Pondering such questions can yield interesting insights and frustrating moral dilemmas. Work, however, requires us to be more practical. Rather than being philosophical, we can take a simple approach by examining karma's influence on how we get the job done.

If, as a child, you enjoyed caring for your toys, keeping them clean and properly stored in boxes or in the closet, you created karma or a *tendency* to keep stuff organized. Keeping closets or desks or drawers neat and clean later in life came a bit easier because you had done such a thing before and it was not out of the ordinary to do it again. Being neat and clean became routine, or a "good" habit. On the other hand, if you noticed someone drop a five-dollar bill on the street and you picked it up and kept it for yourself, you created karma or a *tendency* to steal. Now that you have done such a thing, keeping things that do not belong to you becomes easier. Stealing then becomes routine, or a "bad" habit. According to the laws of karma, keeping our world neat and clean is a helpful tendency and stealing is a harmful tendency.

At work, karmic tendencies have many names: attitudes, procedures, routines, competencies, expertise. These describe ways in which we are predisposed to conduct ourselves, patterns that we follow that bring about results. If we take a moment to examine ourselves, we will notice that we have already developed hundreds of tendencies—work-related behaviors, routines, abilities, and attitudes—some helpful, some not so helpful. Some bring about preferred results; others, results we would rather live without. Respecting karma encourages us to notice carefully that how we develop our routines, skills, and attitudes is something we will be living with for some time to come. If we choose to leave work early but hide that from our manager, we create karma or a tendency to shortchange the situation, making it easier and more likely for us to do so in the future. If we choose to accurately audit our company's tax liabilities, we create karma or a tendency to be honest and trustworthy, making it easier and more likely for us to be so in the future. Fundamentally, respecting karma acknowledges that whatever we do right now in this very moment makes its easier and more likely that we will do more of the same in the future.

Our tendencies to behave in certain ways at work are accompanied by distinct feelings. For example, if for the past ten years you have been building furniture, you have probably developed a natural pace at which you conduct yourself. Handling tools, fitting joints, carrying wood—such habits have a personal feel that you have developed. You may feel spontaneous and at your ease when building furniture. When new challenges come along, you feel comfortable and relaxed enough to adapt and take new approaches. "I could build that table with my eyes closed," you might say, confident in your furniture-building skills. You are not constantly relearning how to use a hammer or how to choose wood. Your woodworking tendencies are so ingrained by now that they feel simple and gratifying and effortless.

In other instances, however, we can become trapped by our tendencies. For example, you may have become resentful toward how you are treated at work. Over the years your manager has asked you to perform tasks that you may feel are beneath you or that you are overqualified for. Maybe on occasion you have been asked to clean the office or order supplies, and you feel put upon. You are excluded from important meetings and your opinion is rarely invited. You have become angry and defensive about your position at work, creating a tendency or attitude with a particularly unpleasant tone. Unlike the effortless pace of woodworking, your defensiveness feels tight and sharp and bitter and a bit out of control. Whenever you are asked to do menial tasks—actually, when your manager asks you to do *anything*—your defensiveness and anger seem to come alive on their own and you become trapped in them, unable to adapt or even think clearly at times. Each new encounter with your manager becomes a distinct threat where you feel a need to defend yourself.

Respecting karma begins with acknowledging these feelings and how they vary with different situations and tendencies. On the one extreme, we have tendencies that seem effortless and natural. We can adapt our attitudes and skills to new circumstances, confident in our abilities. On the other extreme, we have tendencies that seem solid and difficult, where we feel driven by the tight speed of our attitudes and habits, feeling narrow and rigid and unable to adapt. We begin to notice how certain tendencies trap us and others free us; how certain attitudes seem effortless and others strained and tight; how certain routines seem open and adaptable, others rigid and stubborn.

If we examine these feelings underlying our conduct at work, we will discover one of the profound laws of karma: The more we try to defend ourselves, the tighter and more claustrophobic we feel; the more we try to help others or contribute positively to our world, the more we feel open and adaptable. The reason is quite simple: defending ourselves is futile, while helping others or contributing to our world is not. Respecting karma encourages us to be mindful of our tendencies, developing those that make us feel open and adaptable and abandoning those that make us feel tight and claustrophobic.

Developing helpful tendencies or "good" karma can be pretty straightforward. We know it when we feel it. Being courteous, honest, and trustworthy, cultivating *li*, and being decent toward our colleagues at work are central, of course.

Being thorough in our work, responsible in meeting commitments, willing to apply our talents—these too are obvious.
But abandoning "bad" karma or harmful tendencies that make
us defensive and inflexible at work—our arrogance, resentment, greed, laziness, insecurities of all kinds—is much trick-
ier. When we are stiff and self-protective in our attitudes at
work, we tend to have a blind spot, not being aware that our
conduct is unproductive, possibly even abusive. As a result,
becoming aware of our defensiveness can be uniquely difficult.

Yet if we bring our mindfulness to bear on such defensiveness, even for a brief moment, we will discover that our feelings of tightness and resistance are quite sharp and vibrant.
We touch the tone of our personal struggle with our naked
mindfulness, feel the resentment or smugness or fear, and experience our distress directly, without any filters. Inevitably,
our mindfulness reveals that we are trapped by such defensive
tendencies; instinctively, we know that our anxieties are telling us that something is wrong. Respecting karma encourages
us to value such feelings as warnings: "Wake up! Slow down!
Notice where you are! What are you missing?"

Respecting karma reminds us that we have the power to be
decent or corrupt, helpful or selfish, defensive or open every
moment of the day. Each moment we have a choice to put
tendencies in motion that will make it easier to adapt and
be authentic or make it inevitable that we blind ourselves in
defensiveness and worry. We also find ourselves inheriting
tendencies from past choices, some helpful, some not so helpful. By being mindful of our feelings of tightness and claustrophobia or ease and openness, we can slowly abandon our
arrogance, anger, and greed and cultivate ease and well-being
for ourselves and others. By bringing our mindfulness to the
tension and speed of our defensiveness, we can pop the bubble

of our blindness and remind ourselves to wake up and pay attention. And by being mindful of our feelings of ease and flexibility, we can lend a hand to others without resentment, engendering humor and delight among our colleagues.

By respecting karma, we acknowledge that there are no easy answers, no lotteries or guarantees. Rather, we build our world and our character one step at a time, one seed at a time, gradually bearing the fruit of confidence and openness. By respecting karma we make our world more decent both for ourselves and for those around us.

31

Do not-know

ALL OF US WANT to have a purpose at work, and we want to know how to perform our jobs. If we are dishing up ice cream, we want to know how to scoop the correct portions and serve it attractively. If we are repairing the space shuttle, we want to know how to engineer nickel or titanium into protective shields to withstand extreme temperatures. In the most basic way, knowing how to do things at work is what it's all about.

On the other hand, *not knowing* what we are doing at work seems downright unacceptable. If we were to say to our boss or customer, "I don't know what I am doing. I'm not sure I have a handle on the situation," this person could lose confidence in our abilities and might begin to doubt that we are right for the job. If we don't know what we are doing, things could get out of control. Problems of all kinds could arise.

In order to avoid the appearance of such disasters, we generally keep our work-related quandaries to ourselves. Because it is unacceptable to *not know*, we may at times need to pretend we know what we are doing when in fact we don't. Wall Street is great for such charades. On Wall Street, *appearing* to be an expert by talking the part is half the game: matched maturities, on-balance volume, jobbers, continuous net settlement, rising bottoms—the more financial jargon you throw around, the more others assume you know what you are doing. Of course, Wall Street is not the only place where people hide behind jargon. We all, to some degree, feel uncertain at work and try to mask it—to project an image of confidence and know-how.

The fact is that we cannot avoid not knowing; we simply don't know a lot of the time. Because work is messy and full of surprises, we are constantly presented with not knowing what is going on or about to happen. Since this feels uncomfortable and uncertain, we grasp for answers in order to feel sure of ourselves. But being uncomfortable and uncertain need not be seen as a weakness or problem that needs an immediate answer. If we pause and examine closely, we might take the advice offered in the classic Zen teaching "Only don't know" and discover that not knowing is a tremendous resource for being effective and innovative at work.

Cultivating not knowing does not mean that as bus drivers we forget which route to take or to pick up our customers at the bus stop. Nor is it an excuse for being incompetent: "Gee, I don't know how to put paper in the copier; I guess I'll just skip it and find a copier that works." Nor is not knowing a kind of fog where we sit back and vaguely say to ourselves, "What the hell is going on around here?" Rather, not knowing is our willingness to slow down, drop our preconceptions, and be interested and present to our work situation as it unfolds. Not knowing in this sense is an exercise in balancing effort—actively and intelligently *being* somewhere in the process of *getting* somewhere.

Not knowing starts by giving ourselves a break from the

tension of always knowing what to do, the constant accomplishing of something. We shift from the feeling of *making* something happen to *letting* something happen. We relax with our bodies and minds and take a good look at our environment. We no longer cling to what we know and instead become excited about what we don't know. We ease up on the race to get our jobs done and permit ourselves to notice things we don't normally notice. We let our curiosity have a free rein. The family pictures hanging in our colleague's cubicle no longer fade into the background but are colorful and inviting. Our subordinate's frequent use of "Excuse me, I'm sorry but . . ." no longer goes routinely by, simply overlooked as a worn-out phrase. Our client's lawyer's habit of looking at her watch becomes intriguing. The crack in a metal beam, the joy in a voice, the incorrect date on a form letter—all become available and potentially of interest.

Not knowing is highly inquisitive, an energetic curiosity that inspects and questions without being rude or disrespectful. Here we are not curious in order to prove a point or place blame or fix a problem; rather, there is a feeling that our work situation is inviting and crisp—maybe even vast and profound—and worthy of our attention. By not knowing, we give ourselves permission to wander and observe, becoming interested in seeming incidentals that could yield helpful insights.

In the eighties, Wall Street firms measured everything: percent of trades settled in twenty-four hours, average turnaround time for stock swaps, percent of margin calls settled on time; the list was infinite. Management "knew" what was going on, sometimes up to the second. Despite such attention to detail—or maybe because of it—some vital issues went overlooked.

One of my consulting assignments at the time required that

I interview employees in a 120-person "reorg department" to find out why people were going over to the competition in droves—50 percent annual turnover. During an informal tour of the floor, everything *seemed* routine—people were busy and generally amiable. The atmosphere was chaotic but quite focused. I noticed a middle-aged woman off in the corner who, at first glance, blended in perfectly with the setting—but her desk seemed a bit too neat and her composure too relaxed. I asked to interview her and was told that she was "just the department secretary," who had been with the company for thirty-one years, had little to do with the daily function of the department, and really wasn't at risk of leaving. There were more-critical managers and employees to interview.

As I got to know people in the department a bit, I found that one of the conditions they complained about most bitterly was the lack of water. Summertime in many older Wall Street buildings could be brutal. Air conditioning was often not available on the large, open operations floors, and fans kept air circulating in eighty- to eighty-five-degree temperatures. The only "perk" was cooled spring water: each department had its water cooler, but this department's cooler had been removed. Other items, such as desk fans, calculators, even pencils and yellow pads, were virtually impossible to get—for "budget reasons," people were told. Many considered such conditions a signal to move on to another job.

When I brought this issue to management's attention, they were floored. Budgets were tight, sure, but denying people water and pencils? The managers were beside themselves and wanted to know who had authorized such controls. Her name was Sarah, and she was "just the department secretary," who, after thirty-one loyal years with the company, blended in with a desk that was just a bit too neat—and had a deep desire to control.

In a very real sense, the problem was not Sarah but management's inability to "not know" about the conditions in the department. As far as management was concerned, 95 percent of the trades were being settled in under twenty-four hours, so they knew the department was fine. Ironically, this knowing had blinded them. People were leaving, not because they didn't have water or pencils, but because the managers, by thinking they knew what was going on, were, in fact, out of touch, announcing loud and clear: *we are neglecting you; you are not valued.* The managers would not have overlooked such a message if they had permitted themselves to not know on occasion. They might have paid closer attention to the expense reports they were signing, authored by Sarah, who was doing such a great job at controlling costs and depriving employees of water.

The reminder "Do not-know" encourages us to ease up on our speed to constantly be an expert at our job, to shift from making something happen to letting something happen. We can permit our work setting to become available to us, allowing our intelligence and natural curiosity to have free rein. Rather than resisting not knowing, we can relax with it as a natural and necessary part of work. We can allow ourselves the opportunity to appreciate, listen, and observe and be curious about the incidentals, routines, surprises, and even the irritations of our work rather than taking them for granted or being put off by them. We can afford to listen for the unspoken messages, often unintentionally sent and even more often misunderstood. By not knowing, we open up, and so does the world around us, offering an untapped wealth of insight and guidance.

32

Be humble while ambitious

IT IS NATURAL to be determined and motivated at work. We all want to achieve our goals, no matter how modest or grand they may be. Maybe we stay late with our colleagues to put the finishing touches on an important presentation. Or maybe we want to make salesperson of the year and we rehearse our sales strategy thoroughly to make sure every detail is managed properly. Such an approach to work can be quite satisfying. Our ambition to excel and perform our jobs well feels fresh and rewarding, and we don't mind putting in extra effort to succeed. Yet if our drive to be successful becomes out of balance, we can find ourselves feeling confined and overpowered by our ambition, possibly even obsessed. In such instances, when our need for success becomes too intense, we are said to be suffering from "blind ambition."

"Blind ambition" is considered blind because in our rush to succeed we ignore our world. We become so addicted to getting somewhere fast that actually living our lives becomes a constant problem. We may be so wrapped up in our need to achieve that we forget to share success with others or recognize their contributions. Our drive may be so intense that we ignore our own needs. Maybe our health suffers because we focus on nothing but our work, or our family becomes resentful because we are blind to them, superficially involved with their lives but not really available. Or we can become so blinded by our ambition that we feel entitled to ignore rules, such as accounting and ethics guidelines. When we are blind to our world in this way, we become profoundly out of touch with the results of our actions, creating enormous confusion for ourselves and others.

It is difficult to explore our heart and mind when we are blinded by our ambition. Pausing a moment to feel the texture of our experience seems quite out of the question. We therefore misunderstand most of the signals we are receiving. We misread our colleagues' irritation as "just whining" and our exhaustion as the result of a "job well done." Criticism is considered sour grapes. Demanding questions from auditors? Mere stop signs on our road to achievement. Our blindness conceals the facts, including our own desperation.

For blind ambition's bottom line is that we are trapped in a distressing cycle of hope and fear. We are driven by the arrogant desire to conquer our work and the poverty-stricken fear that we may be conquered by it. Unspoken yet obvious, ignored yet fueling our every act, our arrogance and impoverishment hijack our sense of enthusiasm and blind us to being genuinely who we are, where we are. In the end we become so out of balance, so addicted to our hope of getting somewhere fast, that we increasingly misinterpret our situation, becoming lost and confused in our search for success.

Ambition at work need not become blind, however. We can be awake at work and still strive to achieve our goals and do our work well. We can be determined and enthusiastic without losing ourselves at work. Such an approach requires, however, that we balance our ambition to get somewhere with *being humble*.

When we think of being humble, we may imagine ourselves as shy and retiring or quiet when praised. We would be modest and self-deprecating if we were asked to come to the stage and receive the "employee of the century" award. Asked to say a few words, we would do exactly that, saying very little other than that we are not worthy. Such an image of humbleness underestimates the toughness of truly being humble. Being humble is not being a wet noodle. Rather, to be humble is to be willing to deal thoroughly with the details of work, to be patient and careful when managing work's demands. Work's details and messiness are not beneath us; they are not intrusions, annoyances, malfunctions, or inconveniences. Work's details are, in fact, how we live our lives at work—mindfully present and respectfully engaged.

When we are being humble, we are not rushing past the present moment out of feelings of pride or greed. We are willing to engage work's uncertainties and surprises in the present moment. By doing so, we cultivate a quiet and profound understanding of how work influences our life. Our job, our livelihood, the colleagues we work with, the projects we manage, the paycheck we receive, the boss we listen to—all are perfectly arranged to teach us what we need to know in order to wake up and be authentic. And because we appreciate such a thing, we can be grateful, respecting and deeply valuing our circumstances. Preparing properly for our business review, attending to detailed expense reports, patiently handling the customer-service problems, carefully reviewing clinical trial results, become our spiritual path. To be humble is to quietly and thoroughly work with such things, taking the small, practical steps that blind ambition often dismisses as mere annoyances. In such discipline we find a wakeful and fluid ambition that is not hijacked by the arrogance of hope and the hesitation of fear.

Being humble while ambitious reminds us to "balance the two efforts" in our determination and enthusiasm at work, to anchor our effort to get somewhere in being somewhere. By being humble in such a manner, we become grateful to our work setting because it is our opportunity to build a sane and decent world.

"Be humble while ambitious" reminds us quite simply: It is good to know where you are going, so you don't end up in the wrong place. But if you are not humble enough to appreciate and respect where you are, you are probably lost already.

33

Notice and cut work's speed

WORK CAN BE fast and relentless: pressing deadlines, looming goals, endless meetings; e-mail, phone calls, "to do" lists. At times we can feel out of control, as if driving a car with no brakes, rushing through our jobs, holding on around difficult turns, cutting corners, racing through an occasional red light. Just maneuvering through the day seems an accomplishment, leaving us stunned by the franticness of it all. We might even say to ourselves at the end of the day: "Hey, what just happened—I just spent my whole day at a job without noticing any of it!"

If we examine such busyness closely, we notice that it acts like an anesthesia that numbs us from experiencing the present moment. We are constantly in a hurry to get somewhere: busy fighting fires, reacting to emergencies, anticipating what's next, rushing to meet a deadline. Sometimes we can feel composed at such speed—controlled and decisive. Other times we are more reckless and frenzied—impatient even over incidentals. Our speed keeps us unavailable to our world and ourselves, hurrying past the present moment, anesthetized by our jobs. But ironically, the very speed that numbs us at work can also wake us up if we are mindful.

When we sit in meditation, we are inevitably confronted with the very same restless mind that is behind the steering wheel at work. In meditation, however, we simply sit and notice this: our constant mental chatter, our longing to be somewhere else, our antsy-ness for entertainment. Then we bring our attention back to the present moment. By being mindful of our restlessness, we can actually cut through it and wake up. In sitting, we routinely notice and cut speed over and over again. Our restlessness and speed remind us in a very subtle way to let go and *be*.

In the same way, when we are mindful of our job's speed and hecticness, we take a subtle step: we have to actually slow down in order to notice how fast we are going. By simply observing the speed mindfully, we have tapped the brakes, so to speak, and slowed down just a bit. We have noticed there is a speedometer in the car; we have noticed where we are for just a moment. By deliberately acknowledging our restlessness we get the first hint that maybe we are the author of our speed, not just a victim of an out-of-control job.

Many techniques are offered in this book for noticing and cutting work's speed: practicing small boredoms, opening, being kind to yourself, even cultivating the art of conversation. Here, however, what is recommended is actually a form of jujitsu, where one uses the power of one's opponent to gain victory over him or her. The very hecticness that seems to entrap us becomes our foremost reminder to slow down, let go, and regain a balanced and open composure.

At times, noticing and cutting work's speed can be a central leadership challenge. I remember once being asked to attend a meeting with the company's CEO to review the progress of a multimillion-dollar acquisition bid and to review some compensation plans. Since I was invited at the last minute, I was in a bit of a rush to get my papers together and prepare for the meeting. I was unfamiliar with these types of business discussions and felt anxious and off balance.

As I entered the boardroom, several people were busy tapping away on their laptops, a phone was ringing insistently, a senior financial person was talking out loud while glancing over a memo, and the receptionist was handing notes to two people who seemed alarmed by what they were reading. So much was happening at such a hurried pace! As I seated myself, everything seemed to be in the foreground, loud and self-absorbed, vying for my attention like a three-ring circus.

Suddenly the CEO who had called the meeting walked into the room and said: "Okay, who wants to bet? I bet our bid is accepted within twenty-four hours." Seemingly out of nowhere the speed and chaos that were so crowding the foreground were cut and a background of space appeared. Everyone stopped tapping at computers, answering phones, reading notes, speaking out loud, and suddenly confronted a simple question: Who was willing to bet? Suddenly there was tremendous room to breathe and be. It struck me at the time that the CEO had deliberately decided to cut through the chaos with some humor. The speed in the boardroom had alerted him to slow everything down, and he did so quite simply.

We may not have the authority to sweep into a meeting and redirect everyone's attention away from the speed of the moment, but we can, when confronted with work's pressures, tap the brakes and rediscover the sharp clarity of the present moment. Taking a sip of water or offering the same to others, pausing to take a deep breath, smiling or simply saying "good morning," can go a long way toward cutting work's speed. By making such gestures over and over again, we find that our job is not out of control; we are fully equipped with brakes to slow us down, a horn to alert others, headlights to guide us, and mirrors to check. We gradually discover that rather than being reckless, we can be resourceful under pressure, as long as we notice where we are.

Some of us may be able to notice and cut work's speed even at eighty miles an hour, while others may be able to do so only at more modest speeds. But if we consistently and intentionally notice work's speed, we become aware in our hecticness that we are making choices: some frenzied and unskillful, others intelligent and effective. We may be, for example, impulsively trying to solve a problem that should probably remain unsolved for the time being. Maybe our hastily offered opinions serve our need to be heard more than our team's need to solve a pressing problem. Worse, maybe we are thoughtlessly prescribing a drug as an expression of our hurry rather than for the good of our patient. Noticing and cutting work's speed helps us winnow out reckless impulse from decisive clarity, panic from confidence. Like the CEO, we start to notice that much of what is rushed is unnecessary and can be redirected in order to create some room to be. We begin to appreciate, at a very basic level, our ability to manage work, not just get through it. As we pause more and more in the midst of work's franticness, our ability to accomplish work and not be victimized by it becomes increasingly apparent. We begin to value deliberateness over the urge to just "get it done," clear communication over rushing to get our point made, effective planning over mindless routine. In the midst of work's chaos and speed, we develop the composure to rely on ourselves more and more.

Of course, just noticing how demanding and hectic our job

is doesn't necessarily slow that momentum at all. "Notice and cut work's speed" does not suggest that we can escape the reality that work is crowded with deadlines, surprises, and pressure. It simply points out that we need not surrender our awareness in such circumstances, that work's franticness need not numb us to ourselves and our world. Even when pressures are at a fevered pitch, we can pause and be mindful in the immediate moment, permitting work's speed to wake us up rather than put us to sleep.

34

Take a fresh glimpse and adapt

IT IS FITTING that we rely on routines at work. We have schedules, work procedures, and standards that we follow. By making work somewhat predictable in this way, we can be effective in getting the job done, meeting our commitments, and being responsible to our colleagues. Many of our daily work routines contain tremendous wisdom, developed over many generations. How we engineer tension into metals, recognize legal ownership, or manage a seaport all rely on routines that thousands of people before us worked hard to perfect. In that sense, many of the routines that we count on each day are worthy of our respect and careful consideration. There is much to appreciate in how a bridge is built or a heart is transplanted.

Yet, because work is messy and uncertain, our routines are always encountering surprises. A new manager, a modification in an operating system, a warehouse fire, a misprint in an instruction manual, all require that we rethink what is customary and possibly even discard our routines altogether. Our constantly changing workplace demands that we regularly take a fresh glimpse and reinvent how we work.

Ironically, we sometimes rely on our routines when we least need them. When work's surprises require us to adapt and innovate, we can find ourselves instead reaching for familiar habits, making us ineffective or even counterproductive. Sending our new boss the same weekly sales report we have been using for the past five years may not be what she needs or wants. Continuing to ship product "first order in/first order out" during an inventory crisis only makes the disaster worse. Painting the predictable rosy picture of corporate earnings to assure shareholders when we ourselves are far from being assured is irresponsible and reckless. In such cases, instead of adapting and being resourceful, we freeze up and behave habitually, holding on to the status quo, trying to maintain some order in the midst of chaos. The more we hold on to our routines, the more our work evolves out of our control, becoming increasingly stressful and confusing. The status quo becomes a prison, and our routines, millstones around our neck.

Needless to say, becoming imprisoned by work's routines is unnecessary. Adapting to surprises and chaos need not be a monumental task but a simple shift from holding on to letting go, from maintaining a point of view to not having one at all, from trying to solve a problem to listening for solutions, from remaining convinced to taking a fresh glimpse and adapting.

At the heart of such a shift is our willingness, at any given moment, to let go of our habits and fixed views and suddenly become available to our work setting, permitting circumstances to unfold. It is at that very moment that we take a fresh glimpse and adapt. Such a glimpse has no agenda other than to better understand and appreciate the immediate moment. When we become available to our circumstances in this way, we are naturally curious, wondering how this or that works, appreciating how a particular opinion is expressed, or marveling at the scope of a problem or the elegance of a solution. When we permit ourselves to be present and available, we experience a heightened awareness, a sharp, unburdened intelligence that is open and pliable yet firm.

This curiosity or awareness is not passive but active. Since we are not burdened by maintaining a point of view, we naturally ask questions, probe, and clarify. In taking a fresh glimpse and adapting, we invite the wisdom of others; we seek out good judgment, helpful insights, experienced advice, novel approaches—listen, listen, and listen again. We stop trying to make something happen and instead let something happen, learning as we go. By being open and willing in this way, we can then innovate with confidence. Adapting to work's surprises is not a one-man show: if we "adapt" only for ourselves by ourselves, it is more often than not an exercise in holding on to the status quo, and not adaptation at all. We include others as we adapt; we experiment with new approaches that meet others' needs and not just our own. Rather than sending our new boss a standard weekly sales report, we discuss with her first what would be best, adapting our approach to hers. Rather than shipping product "first order in/first order out" during our inventory crisis, we speak with all the regional sales directors and build a priority customer list for shipping orders, adapting our approach to the teams. Rather than painting the predictable rosy picture of corporate earnings, we seek views and opinions from our managers, build a consensus among top executives, and bring a balanced and shared view to the shareholders, adapting our approach to build commitment among many.

"Take a fresh glimpse and adapt" reminds us to respect our routines without becoming trapped by them when work's surprises require us to be flexible. By letting go of our familiar habits and routines and "not knowing," we discover that we can trust our natural intelligence to engage work as it unfolds, seeking out novel approaches to unknown circumstances. Being mindful and available during work's surprises heightens our curiosity, and we naturally seek out the wisdom of others. We include others as we change, flexible enough to embrace many viewpoints, not just our own.

35

Keep your seat

IN ANCIENT JAPAN, certain samurai lords would lead their troops by taking a position on a hill above them, overlooking the field where battle was to take place. Here the lord would set up his headquarters. With colorful tents and flags and military personnel coming and going, the regal encampment was designed to give a formidable impression. As the moment approached for battle, the lord would have a stool or bench placed at the crest of the hill. There, in full battle armor and armed with swords, he would take his seat in full view of his and the enemy's troops, his clan banner planted firmly at his side. A few feet behind the lord to his left knelt a single attendant, he too armed for battle.

As the skirmish formed and the armies engaged, the lord would remain seated, observing the unfolding events. The initial dueling of archers, the series of cavalry charges, the flanking foot soldiers wielding long spears attempting to unseat enemy horsemen—the lord would watch the entire display, following plans as they unfolded and individual warriors as they performed their duty. No matter what the circumstances, the lord would *keep his seat* through the entire fray, sometimes for days, remaining within view of his troops throughout the battle.

Sometimes the disciplined troop movements and imaginative strategies would prove effective and victory would appear to be emerging. Then, with a surge from the enemy, a line of defense would break and the tide would turn. At times the enemy might fight within striking distance of the lord, and his troops would battle fiercely to prevent him from being harmed. Still the lord would not be swept away to safety, nor would he run for his life: he would keep his seat like a mountain, his attention and heart never wavering from his troops and the battle.

If all became lost and the lord's troops were defeated, he would take his own life. He would not retreat to safety. In some instances, if it seemed he was about to be overrun and killed, his attendant would rise and swiftly, with a single sword stroke, remove the lord's head—as the lord had commanded him before battle. Under all circumstances the lord would keep his seat.

The lord's poise and bravery were said to be enormously inspiring to the samurai engaged in combat. During the battle, each warrior could glance toward his lord and see that he was keeping his seat and know that his fierce spirit was alive and with him, carefully observing, remaining alert and composed. The warriors could draw on such strength of heart and martial will, and their mutual loyalty with their lord would provoke them to engage battle with a continued confidence and discipline. The enemy too would be well aware of the lord's poise and the effect it was having on their adversaries. They too would sense the power of such a presence keeping his seat coolly and fiercely on the crest of the hill.

Most of our jobs, of course, fall short of pitched battles among samurai. We may work with a cranky colleague who carries a fingernail clipper in his briefcase or a competitor who is perpetually undercutting our prices, but there is no atten- dant behind our desk ready to lop off our head. Nor are there thousands of troops fighting to the death at our command. Yet, like the samurai lord, we too may want to cultivate our ability to keep our seat at work, to remain brave, alert, and precise under all circumstances.

In order to keep our seat, we must first understand what inspires us to do so. Maybe we keep our seat in order to protect our territory, determined to defend our job or title or prestige under all circumstances. Keeping our seat in this way makes us feel suspicious rather than alert, and stubborn rather than confident. Or we may keep our seat in order not to flinch, like the game of chicken where we test our will against another's to see who cringes first. We keep a poker face, never letting on how we truly feel. We don't wince when we lose the fourteen- million-dollar deal. We don't jump up and down and cheer when we are promoted to CEO; we don't want anyone to know how deeply we desired the promotion. By keeping our seat in such a way, we feel smug rather than confident, enter- tained rather than precise, detached and unavailable rather than composed.

In order to be awake at work, we cannot keep our seat merely out of stubbornness or as a game of chicken. Rather, we keep our seat because to do so is to be who we are where we are. In the Buddhist tradition, such conviction is developed by quite literally keeping our seat in meditation. When we keep our seat on a cushion, we are not actually challenged by fierce samurai armies or difficult business problems. We face a different challenge: to keep our seat whether we are relaxed or tense, cold or warm, cheerful or sad, rich or poor, healthy or distressed, young or old. We may keep our seats in meditation because we are scared or stubborn at first, then later because we don't want to flinch. But at some point, by sitting on a cushion, we discover that we are keeping our seat because we are basically fine *as we are where we are*. We discover our authenticity and that our confidence, alertness, and precision depend on nothing other than our willingness to be who we are where we are.

Developing authentic conviction is extraordinarily powerful because we establish how to *be* before exploring what to *do*. Such an approach reveals that we have already profoundly succeeded before engaging any activity. Whether it's running a business or driving a taxi, performing surgery or mowing a lawn, keeping our seat already accomplishes a major part of the task: determining how we are going to *be*. As a result, we do not lose our composure and power in a rush to do something or be someone other than who we are. Our confidence, alertness, and precision arise naturally by simply and bravely being who we are where we are—without waiting for circumstances to confirm or deny our state of mind. As situations arise, whether disappointing or rewarding, surprising or predictable, we act from our own innate courage, alert to shifting circumstances, precise in our words and deeds and confident in being thoroughly present and available.

Keeping our seat in such a way brings the courage and wisdom of the ancient samurai to our livelihood. It is said that the samurai masters who had firmly established how to be before engaging battle had developed a vast point of view called the all-victorious mind: a mind whose victory was timeless whatever the outcome of combat. Today, by keeping our seat on the cushion, at work, and throughout our lives, we too may discover the same "all-victorious" truth about our mind: that being who we are where we are is unlimited, endowing us with a courage that never fades.

APPENDIXES

INSTRUCTIONS FOR
MINDFULNESS-AWARENESS MEDITATION

SITTING MEDITATION is a friendly gesture toward ourselves in which we take time simply to be. The mindfulness developed in the practice naturally unfolds on the job, guiding us to be authentic, precise, and decent. Sitting down and being still is at the heart of being awake at work. Such meditation cannot be rushed or forced, so we need not hurry; we can be flexible with ourselves and our life circumstances as we learn this practice.

Posture

When we sit, we take a posture sitting upright, relaxed and alert. Our eyes are open, with a soft gaze; our hands are placed palms down, gently resting on our thighs. Our chin is tucked in and our gaze is slightly downward. Our face and jaw are relaxed and our mouth is slightly open. We breathe normally and sit still. If we are sitting on the floor, we sit on a cushion with our legs loosely crossed. Or we may choose to sit on a chair with our feet firmly on the ground. Under all circumstances our posture remains the same: upright and relaxed.

Thinking and Labeling

When we sit, we have two distinct experiences. First, we notice the simple vividness of our immediate circumstances: the faint sound of passing traffic, the color of our rug, the light pressure of our hands on our thighs, the soft smell of incense. For a moment our senses become sharply alive and our experience in the immediate moment becomes uncomplicated and simple.

Second, we also notice that we are thinking: talking to ourselves, commenting on any number of things. Particularly if we are sitting for the first time, we may find ourselves unusually restless with our thoughts. Such restlessness is not a problem; it is what we work with in sitting.

Attending to these two experiences—being alert in the immediate moment and thinking—is central to sitting practice, and working with them properly requires a precise yet gentle awareness of the breath. The next instruction for sitting meditation, then, is when you notice yourself thinking to silently say "thinking" and then bring your attention gently to your out-breath. You, in effect, label the thought "thinking" and bring your attention back to *now*.

Attending to the Breath

Attending to the out-breath in such a way requires patience and vigilance. Particularly at the beginning we may find our minds wandering and rarely attending to our out-breath. By patiently doing the practice, however, the mind begins to rest with the out-breath. We find that we can keep our attention on our out-breath like gently running our hand over a piece of silk. Slowly, precisely, again and again, we gently place our attention on our out-breath and eventually find balance where we are mindful both of our breath and of the immediate moment.

*　*　*

The meditation instruction presented here is called *mind-fulness-awareness*, or *sitting*, meditation and it comes from the Tibetan Kagyu-Nyingma Buddhist tradition. This instruction is enough to get started, and it could even be all you'll ever need. But most likely that will not be the case. As you go further into a daily meditation practice, questions and obstacles will arise, which is quite natural. Traditionally, it is recommended that meditators receive face-to-face instructions from another person qualified to teach mindfulness-awareness meditation. This way you can get fuller instruction, try it out, and ask questions based on your experiences. See my Web site, www.AwakeAtWork.net, for a list of nationwide centers where you can receive meditation instruction.

Generally you will want to cultivate a regular sitting practice, keeping to a schedule each day. At first, fifteen minutes in the morning or evening will be ample time, but gradually you will want to extend your practice, sitting thirty, forty, or perhaps sixty minutes a day. But it's important to begin where you can, not to force yourself. You can extend the time of your sitting period naturally rather than feeling pushed or obliged. It is recommended that you set aside an area to meditate, uncluttered and free from distractions. Choosing to buy a meditation cushion and other accessories is fine, but sitting on a chair or stool is fine as well.

The instructions given here are deceptively simple, so I encourage you to take your time and work with them gradually and wholeheartedly.

INSTRUCTIONS FOR
CONTEMPLATING THE SLOGANS

GENERALLY SPEAKING, these slogans are meant to be applied as a "contemplation-in-action," in which we permit our mindfulness to mingle freely with life's circumstances on the job. However, it also is appropriate to set aside time to contemplate work's challenges more deliberately. By reflecting on work's challenges in such a way, we can slow the turbulence of our mind and cultivate our innate wisdom. Like permitting cloudy water to rest and gradually become clear, contemplation eases work's daily speed and gently allows our *li* and authenticity to shine.

1. *Choose a peaceful setting.* Choose a physical setting that is soothing and calm. You may choose to stroll along a wooded path, sit quietly in a shrine room or church, or simply have a cup of tea at your kitchen table.

2. *Be mindful.* Take a moment to let go of your inner dialogue and appreciate your immediate surroundings. Simply notice the sights and sounds and appreciate the quiet openness of the moment. Mindfulness meditation for five minutes or so is recommended.

3. *Recall the purpose.* We do not contemplate in order to gratify our hopes or dispel our fears. By contemplating work's circumstances, we are acknowledging our resourcefulness and

authenticity and choosing to consider decent and skillful actions. Try this short verse:

> *Without hope and without fear,*
> *May I be decent in my actions,*
> *May I be helpful to others.*

4. *Invite and consider the object of contemplation.* If you have a particular issue at work you wish to explore, bring this to mind. Let the mind and heart freely and curiously consider the ideas and images that arise: recall workplace experiences, consider "what ifs," assess risks and rewards, feel excitements or distress thoroughly. At some point, read a slogan, either randomly or deliberately. Note any emotions and physical feelings that accompany the topic and write down any particularly helpful ideas or suggestions that come to mind. Be gently mindful of any tingling in the stomach, heaviness in the chest, or tightness in the throat throughout the contemplation. Permit these feelings to inform you as you mix the slogan with the contemplation of your work circumstances.

5. *Note any shifts and conclude with an aspiration.* Not all contemplation offers a clear and final resolution, though at times this can be the result. It is likely, however, that our view of work may have changed during our moment of reflection. Where once there was anger, hesitation, or resistance, there may now be relief, resolve, or sadness. Such a shift in view or feeling may inspire us to conduct ourselves differently. You may choose to end the contemplation by writing down an intention, any new behavior or course of action you intend to take because of the contemplation. For example, after

contemplating "Practice 'no credentials,'" you may aspire to be more aware of the people providing you a service at the grocery store, cleaners, or tollbooth. By ending our contemplation in this way, we can then aspire to bring a fresh perspective to the job.

CONTEMPLATIONS-IN-ACTION ON WEALTH

WHILE CONTEMPLATION can often be a moment of quiet inner reflection, the contemplations suggested below require action. Listening to advice, preparing a meal, giving away a lottery ticket—all are designed to widen our view of what wealth *really* is and could be. I recommend that you keep notes when doing these contemplations and experiments. Engage the world on its terms and simply listen and learn.

Widen your perspective with research. Often our view of wealth is very "me" centered. What will happen to me if my savings run out? Now that I am rich, I can do what I always wanted to! If only I had more savings, I could retire early. We can get a larger perspective by quantifying how millions of others live their lives. For example, we could research local county government records to find out that 4,596 elderly men and women live on welfare in our local community. We could use the Internet to discover that our salary and savings make us richer than 6.17 billion or 98.3 percent of all the other people in the world. Log each fact in a common file for future reference and reflection. By researching and contemplating such facts, we widen our view of wealth, leading us to open our heart and consider others.

Ask for help. Just as Dr. John Coleman, former president of the Federal Reserve Bank of Philadelphia (see "Practice 'no credentials'"), traveled the country listening to others in order to learn how to make good monetary policy, we can do the same. You may choose to visit someone in a nursing home, ask advice from a homeless woman, call your multimillionaire college roommate, or maybe just visit with your mom or dad to ask for help. Have a deliberate question(s) in mind before you call or visit. For example, if you intend to ask help from a homeless person, you may want to ask: "What advice do you have for people who have a lot of money?" or "What three lessons have you learned from life that you think could help me?" Each interview should be documented and logged in a common file for future reference and contemplation.

Make an offering. Essential to contemplating wealth is understanding the way we express it. The suggestions below are actually exercises in mindfulness-awareness and being authentic in which we express our sense of dignity and richness by offering to others.

- Prepare and serve a meal for your family or friends on a budget of only five dollars per person. Pay special attention to presentation and atmosphere.
- Purchase a tasteful and modestly priced item (for example, a tie, scarf, desk ornament), wrap it elegantly, and present it to a friend or acquaintance.
- Place an arrangement of fresh flowers in a prominent place in your office.
- Dress in your finest suit or dress and visit a museum, preferably with a friend who also is performing this contemplation-in-action. Keep your pace and state of mind simple and unhurried. Keep discussion to a minimum. Before you leave, choose one objet d'art of particular appeal and mindfully appreciate it and the surroundings for ten to fifteen minutes.

- While at a museum, purchase three to five appealing cards from the gift shop. Use them within one week to write a brief note to a friend, family member, or acquaintance.
- Take a silent walk in the woods or in a park. Locate a pleasant area that catches your eye, perhaps beneath a tree or next to a stream. Take a seat and appreciate your surroundings for ten to twenty minutes. Possibly practice mindfulness meditation. Leave behind a small gift such as a coin, brass button, or strip of colorful cloth in an appropriate spot.

Play with money's power. We almost always treat money as a precious item: keeping it safe in our wallets, counting it carefully, putting it in savings accounts. Here we purposefully "play" with money, being sharply mindful of the conflicting emotions and insights such play provokes.

- Purchase a lottery ticket, place it in an envelope, and mail it to a randomly selected address or place it in a randomly selected book in a bookstore. Notice how your mind reacts to giving away a chance at winning.
- Take two to five fresh, large bills—one-hundred-dollar bills if you can afford it, twenty- or ten-dollar bills if you can't. Seal them in a clean white envelope, place the envelope on your dressing table, and see how long you can refrain from opening the envelope and spending the money. Notice sharply what feelings arise each time you see the envelope.
- Go for a walk in the city with no money, credit cards, or checkbook. Notice any urges to purchase

food, drink, or other items. When you realize that you can't make a purchase, what are you left with? How do you feel?

- Seal as many two-dollar bills as you can afford (not to exceed twenty-five) individually into clean white envelopes. Leave them anywhere you want or give them away to anyone you choose within two hours. Notice any uneasiness. Note carefully your choices.

- Purchase from a bank a stack of newly minted one-dollar bills. Keep the bills in their original wrapper and keep them with you wherever you go—in your briefcase, purse, or backpack. Refrain from spending any of the bills for seven days. Notice any feelings that arise each time you see the neatly stacked bills.

Contemplate abundance. By defining wealth as *having an abundance of what we value most,* we shift our focus from money to living life. Take the time to write down one to three aspects of life that you value most and then launch a campaign for thanking those who have helped you in those regards.

If "friendship and family" is high on your list, plan a party and invite all your friends and family members to the event. If "just being alive" appears on your list, visit your mom and dad and thank them for bringing you into the world. If "spirituality" is high on your list, pay a special visit to your priest, pastor, rabbi, or spiritual teacher to express your appreciation. Or visit your most respected sacred place and make a heartfelt offering. If "learning" is on your list, send a letter to the teachers or authors you most admire. If "art" is on your list, support a "struggling artist" with words of encouragement or more practical support.

FIVE CONTEMPLATIONS
FOR CULTIVATING *LI*

CULTIVATING *li* starts with trusting that our minds and hearts are inherently decent. When we are free from resentment, greed, and fear, we instinctively know how to behave properly and wholesomely. Yet such natural decency must be appreciated and developed; it cannot be taken for granted. The following contemplations are designed to help cultivate *li* and strengthen our natural sense of decency on the job.

Contemplate the impact of fear. The single greatest obstacle to cultivating *li* is fear. Fear of losing our job, of being embarrassed or sidelined, of uncertainty, of conflict—fear at work clouds our natural instinct to behave properly. Instead we worry and blame and protect ourselves. Recognizing fear in the workplace, then, is a central exercise in understanding how *li* is corrupted at work. The secretary intimidated by a screaming boss is learning *not* to be honest; the systems analyst rushing to meet another oppressive deadline is learning *not* to trust management; the accountant who is told to "just approve" the clearly inappropriate salary increase is learning *not* to have integrity. By acknowledging and reflecting on these instances at work, our conviction to be honest with ourselves and cultivate *li* can grow.

Contemplate how you bend the truth. How many times have we bent, colored, or dressed up the truth? Saying, "I've been waiting for half an hour!" knowing it's been only about twenty minutes. Or "I saved the company about five hundred thousand dollars with that project," knowing that the final cost savings was never really tallied up. Or "I sent the check out Thursday," knowing Friday afternoon was more like it. Being aware of how we stretch the truth in order to protect ourselves or to project our own story line is an excellent contemplation on how we corrupt *li*. As we notice our "white lies" we can also be intently aware of the inner awkwardness and physical anxiety that accompany such maneuvers. We can then refrain from such dishonesty and be authentic instead, relying on a basic confidence that is fresh and straightforward.

Contemplate the integrity of others. There are always people who inspire us at work. The manager who openly takes responsibility for a problem that others seem to be walking away from; the customer who returns the five-dollar bill the waitress mistakenly included in the change; the politician who refuses to sugarcoat difficult news. *Li* is actually manifested millions of times a day by millions of people around the world. By recognizing such acts of integrity and appreciating the strength of character and fresh decency exhibited by others, we enliven *li* within ourselves.

Review and contemplate your company's code of ethical conduct. Most companies have a code of ethical conduct that is readily available to all employees. While no code can substitute for *li*, contemplating the strengths and weaknesses of a company's ethical guidelines can offer us insights into how *li* can be better cultivated at work. Obtain a copy, read it carefully, and reflect on its intent and substance. Are the words hollow legalese or do they inspire a vision of decency and wholesomeness? Do people in the company actually adhere to the values or are they just tired expressions that no one pays attention to? If the latter is true, what seems to be holding the company back from instilling the values in the managers and employees of the company? How would you improve the code?

Develop a personal code of business etiquette. Write down your top ten rules for proper conduct at work. Here's a favorite example of mine from a late-nineteenth-century anonymous businessman's personal rules of etiquette: "Never break an engagement when one is made, whether of a business or social nature. If you are compelled to do so, make an immediate apology either by note or in person." Or one of my own: "Take the other's view before making a decision." Keep a copy of your personal code in your calendar, purse, or wallet as a reminder of what you want to cultivate at work.